UFOs

UFOs

A HISTORY OF ALIEN ACTIVITY FROM SIGHTINGS TO ABDUCTIONS TO GLOBAL THREAT

Rupert Matthews

CHARTWELL
BOOKS, INC.

PICTURE CREDITS

Victoria Burt **43**; Corbis **33, 81, 186, 195**; Flickrname 'Pixxiefish' **61**; Flickrname 'Michael' **83**; Getty **25, front and back cover**; Nick Ilott **55**; Brian Kilburn **47**; Mary Evans **10, 21, 30, 40, 62, 66, 68, 75, 76, 84, 88, 90, 119, 130, 131, 133, 137, 144, 161, 162, 196**; Justin Gaurav Murgai **23 br**; photos.com **28, 168**; Shutterstock **6, 22, 23 bl, 50, 53, 70, 114, 159, 199**; William Stoneham **13, 72, 74, 97, 105, 123, 129, 146, 149, 192, 202**; Topfoto **16, 18, 24, 36, 38, 44, 48, 56, 60, 65, 87, 94, 95, 101, 102, 103, 105, 106, 109, 111, 117, 120, 125, 126, 132, 134, 139, 141, 142, 143, 150, 151, 154, 156, 157, 158, 163, 173, 174, 178, 182, 183, 187, 189**; Ed Uthman **23 bm**

This edition printed in 2009 by

CHARTWELL BOOKS, INC.
A Division of **BOOK SALES, INC.**
114 Northfield Avenue
Edison, New Jersey 08837

Copyright © 2009 Arcturus Publishing Limited
26/27 Bickels Yard, 151–153 Bermondsey Street,
London SE1 3HA

ISBN-13: 978-0-7858-2430-5
ISBN-10: 0-7858-2430-8
AD001083EN

Printed in China

CONTENTS

JUST LAST SUMMER I SAW A UFO

I have been investigating, researching and writing about UFOs and aliens for some fifteen years or so now, but never before have I seen something flying in the sky that I could not identify. I have seen odd lights aplenty, but generally close to airports or airfields that would probably explain them. Although I have spoken to plenty of people who have had odd encounters, I had never had one myself. Judging by what witnesses had told me, I was not altogether sorry about this.

Author Rupert Matthews had been investigating UFOs for many years before he had his brush with the unknown.

Port Gaverne Beach, Cornwall, where the author and his family had their unexplained encounter.

But there I was on a beach in Cornwall, England, on a balmy summer's evening, walking back to the holiday cottage that my family and I had rented, after a rather nice meal at a local pub. My friend Pete suddenly stopped and pointed up into the sky.

'What's that?' he asked.

Moving slowly through the sky towards us was a line of red globes. They made no sound, moving with an eerie silence. There were eight of them, all moving at a steady speed and in a straight line – coming from inland and heading out towards the sea. I stopped to watch them, as did my wife and Pete's wife. The objects came steadily onwards, heading more or less straight for us.

It was difficult to gauge their height, size or speed since in the clear night sky of a Cornish summer there was nothing to really compare them to. I would guess that they were not flying very high, perhaps a few hundred feet at most, and that they were quite small, maybe a couple of feet across. Nor did they move very quickly. Perhaps no faster than I could run.

As we watched, the objects reached a point almost overhead, though slightly to the east. The first one came to a gradual stop and then appeared to climb steadily upwards. The second reached about the same spot, then it too halted and began to climb. Moving in silent succession, each of the objects did precisely the same thing. By the time the eighth had come to a stop and begun to climb, the first two or three had faded from view.

For a few moments we watched as the glowing lights climbed. Then the final one faded out of sight. They had gone.

What were they? Well, the easy answer is that I do not know. And for that reason they can be counted as UFOs. They were Unidentified, they were Flying and they were Objects.

I doubt that there was anything very odd about them, however. Cornwall is a holiday destination for teenagers, the elderly and everyone in between. And people on holiday can get up to all sorts of odd things – especially in a place that has always been associated with mystery and adventure.

My personal view is that the objects were most probably a number of those paper balloons that are powered by a small burning lamp suspended underneath them. The hot air from the lamp fills the balloon, causing it to rise into the sky. When let off at

'The second object reached about the same spot, then it too halted and began to climb. Moving in silent succession, each of the objects did precisely the same thing.'

night the balloon is virtually invisible and only the flaming lamp is to be seen, as if suspended in the air.

The movement of the objects that we saw would seem to fit this idea. Several balloons let off from the same spot a minute or so apart would rise up into the sky and follow a similar path. Drifting north on a breeze they may have reached the turbulent airflows that usually form over the coast as the cool sea air is drawn in beneath warm land air columns and rises. That may have been the cause of their sudden halt and steep climb.

Well, that is my idea. When dealing with UFOs it is usually best to propose a mundane explanation whenever possible. But the truth is that we saw so little of the objects that it is impossible to be certain what they were.

And that is very often the problem with reports of UFOs. So many of them are lacking in detail, could be explained as perfectly normal objects or are rather uninteresting. On that basis, sceptics argue that there are no such things as truly unexplained flying objects, there are only ordinary objects in the sky that the witness did not properly identify. Less charitable sceptics would suggest that at least some

A paper hot air balloon with suspended burning lantern. This type of item may have been behind the author's UFO sighting.

witnesses have simply made the whole thing up.

But that is not the case. As this book will show there is much, much more to it than a few glowing fires seen drifting through the summer sky.

Some UFOs are considerably more sinister and dangerous than that.

Rupert Matthews, 2008

AN ALIEN EXPERIENCE

On 15 September 1967, 14-year-old Carol Luke invited her friend Ruth Passini back after school to the Luke farm, which stood a few miles outside Winsted in Connecticut. At about 7.30 pm Carol's mother went out to the shops, saying she would be back in roughly an hour. The two girls went up to Carol's bedroom to listen to music and chat. Around the time that Mrs Luke was due home, Carol glanced out of the window to see if the car headlights were yet in view.

What she saw amazed her.

Sitting on the ground in a pasture field about 200 yds (180 m) away was an egg-shaped object that glowed with an inner light. Carol called Ruth to the window and together they watched as the object pulsated through white to beige to pink to orange and back to white again. At times the glow was bright enough to illuminate the barn that stood between the farmhouse and the pasture, at others it faded until the object could be seen only by the silver light of the three-quarter moon that gleamed down from the sky. The object was, the two girls decided, about the size of a car.

After five minutes or so the object emitted a loud drone for a few seconds, then reverted to silence. As if this were a signal of some kind, two figures emerged from the barn. Their size could be judged clearly by comparison to the barn door. The two figures were a little under 4 ft (1.2 m) tall. They were dressed in identical tight-fitting suits of a darkish colour. Their heads were rather larger than they would

'At times the glow was bright enough to illuminate the barn that stood between the farmhouse and the pasture ... '

have been if they were human children. At first Carol and Ruth thought that the figures were wearing helmets which would have accounted for their unusual head size, but they later decided that the intruders simply had rather large heads.

Having glanced towards the glowing object, the two visitors walked slowly across the farmyard. They paused by the mailbox that stood beside the open gate into the road for some two minutes or so, then crossed the road and vanished into the dark shadow of a large tree. The tree stood in the paddock of a neighbouring house owned by a Mrs Pinozza.

The two girls did not feel threatened in any way. The two figures seemed to be curious rather than dangerous. They seemed to be looking around the farmyard to see what was there. Certainly they made no effort to break into the house or to steal anything. They did not seem to be armed, or even to be carrying anything at all. They did not really do anything much, except to look about the place.

UNINVITED VISITORS

Nevertheless, the two figures had most certainly not been invited to the farm, nor did the girls recognize them as friends or acquaintances. What they had at first thought might be young boys were now seen to be something quite different altogether. They were short humanoids with large heads who were somehow linked to the odd glowing object in the pasture. While neither girl at this point thought the beings to be aliens from another planet, nor did they believe that what they were witnessing was entirely normal.

A short time later, as the two girls discussed what they should do, a pair of headlights appeared in the distance. Hoping that this was Mrs Luke returning from the store, the two girls decided to open the window so that they could call down to her when she got out of the car to warn her of the intruders.

As they did so the two figures re-emerged from the tree, walked briskly back into the farmyard and were joined by a third identical figure. After what seemed to be a hurried discussion about the approaching car, the three figures walked quickly around the barn,

'They were short humanoids with large heads who were somehow linked to the odd glowing object in the pasture.'

apparently heading for the mysterious object. As they disappeared around the corner of the barn, the object faded until it was barely visible.

The approaching car turned out not to be that of Mrs Luke, for it sped past the farm without stopping. As soon as it was out of view the object began to glow

once again. Then it seemed to lift off the ground slightly and move away.

It was at this point that Mrs Luke arrived home. The excited girls dashed down to tell her about the mysterious intruders and to point out the rapidly disappearing object. Mrs Luke saw the glowing egg-shaped vessel travelling into the distance, but by the time she saw it the object could have easily been a low-flying aircraft, so she was at first reluctant to believe what the girls said.

The trio then crossed the road to speak to Mrs Pinozza. The neighbour had, indeed, seen the object resting in the pasture. But she had not seen any diminutive figures. Unlike the two girls she had been so terrified by the strange glowing object that she had locked the doors, slammed the shutters and phoned her husband to demand that he return home as soon as possible.

The following day another neighbour, Bruce Marecki, who lived some distance away, confirmed that he had seen some odd lights over in the direction of the Luke farm but had not paid much attention, thinking them to be fireworks or something similar.

The police were called, the press alerted. For a few days, the Luke farm swarmed with investigators and curious onlookers. Then the excitement faded away. With no clues to follow up the police put the file on hold, and with no subsequent sensations the press soon lost interest. The strange intruders never came back to Winsted, Connecticut. After their short brush

This illustration shows the three aliens and their UFO that visited a remote farm in Connecticut, USA, in 1967.

with the unexplained, Carol Luke and Ruth Passini went back to school and continued with their lives.

And yet something had come to that remote Connecticut farm on a fine September evening in 1967. There were five witnesses to the glowing object, all of whom gave consistent and credible descriptions of what they saw. There is no known natural phenomenon nor artificial aircraft that could accurately replicate what this object looked like and did.

What is more, somebody, or something, spent a good twenty minutes or so looking around the farmyard, crossing to the neighbour's yard and coming back again. Of course, it was only the two teenage girls who saw the three figures – Mrs Pinozza was cowering in her home by the time they appeared – but there is no real need to doubt either their honesty or their eyesight. The girls were known neither for inventing tales nor for misleading adults. Nor did they put forward outlandish descriptions of either the appearance or the behaviour of the unexplained nocturnal visitors. We are left with plenty of questions about these strange visitors. Who were they? Why did they visit? What did they do?

Looking only at the Winsted Incident, it is impossible to answer those questions. No one saw the object arrive, and given that it left by flying out of sight, no one can take even a guess at where it went. Nor did anyone see the three humanoid figures emerge from or disappear into the object, though it seems reasonable to assume that they did both. Certainly they were watched walking towards the object just seconds before it lifted off and they were no longer seen after it had gone. The description of the figures is clear enough, but vague on details. They were just under 4 ft (1.2 m) high and had large heads but were otherwise apparently humanoid with two arms, two legs and a body all of roughly human proportions. Were it not for the strange object, they might have been taken for young boys wearing helmets of some kind.

If there is not enough evidence to tell what the object was or where the humanoids came from, there is even less to indicate what their purpose was. Nothing was found to be missing, nor even noticeably moved about, after the visitors had gone. While the girls thought the intruders had seemed curious about the farmyard and its contents, they had not shown any great interest in any one object or thing. They seemed merely to be taking a look around.

In itself, the Winsted Incident is an enigma that simply cannot be explained. It is not one of the famous UFO incidents and is largely ignored in the generally available literature. Put simply, it is too banal to be of much interest to those researchers who delight in the sensational.

'The visitors, whoever they were, quite clearly did not realize that they were being observed by the two girls.'

And yet in its very ordinariness the Winsted Incident is so valuable. The visitors, whoever they were, quite clearly did not realize that they were being observed by the two girls. When the first car appeared they went to some lengths to get out of sight, and left altogether when Mrs Luke arrived home. The rest of the time they seem to have been behaving as they would have done had they been on the farm alone. Maybe they had seen Mrs Luke leave and thought the farm to be abandoned.

And by studying a mass of such unremarkable and unspectacular sightings it is often possible to learn far more than by looking at only one or two famous examples.

' ... by studying the vast mass of data and sightings available it is possible to build up a composite picture of what is going on ...'

It is a well-known fact that eyewitnesses can be unreliable. Police the world over have to contend with varying descriptions given by different people of the same suspect. A man seen running from a shop during a robbery is unlikely to be described in the same way by everyone who saw him. Rather than give up, the police are adept at looking for common features.

If seven witnesses say the man was blond and only one says he was a redhead, the chances are that he was blond. If three witnesses say he escaped in a blue car, five that he drove off in a Ford and two that the car had a man in the passenger seat in addition to the suspect then it is fairly safe to assume that the suspect escaped in a blue Ford together with an accomplice. Not all the witnesses need to see exactly the same things for a complete picture to be built up.

So it is with the UFO phenomena. No one witness can be expected to get the full picture. Some witnesses will contradict each other. And yet by studying the vast mass of data and sightings available it is possible to build up a composite picture of what is going on that is likely to be as close to the truth as we humans are going to get.

And that truth might be dramatic, surprising and not at all what most people might expect.

The 1947 sighting of strange flying objects by Kenneth Arnold sparked the world's interest in UFOs.

Most UFO books and articles date the phenomenon to the famous 1947 sighting by Kenneth Arnold. This crucial story has been often told, and its main features can be laid out quite quickly.

On 24 June 1947 Arnold, a highly experienced pilot, was flying his private aircraft over the Cascade Mountains of Washington State. His attention was caught by a flash of light, such as that caused by the sun flashing off the polished wings of another aircraft. Idly glancing in that direction he was amazed to see a formation of nine strange aircraft flying at extraordinary speed. The craft were crescent-shaped, bright silver in colour and flying in a military-style echelon formation. As they moved the craft did not fly in a straight line, but bobbed or skipped along.

The idea that these objects were alien spacecraft, ghosts or anything at all paranormal did not occur to

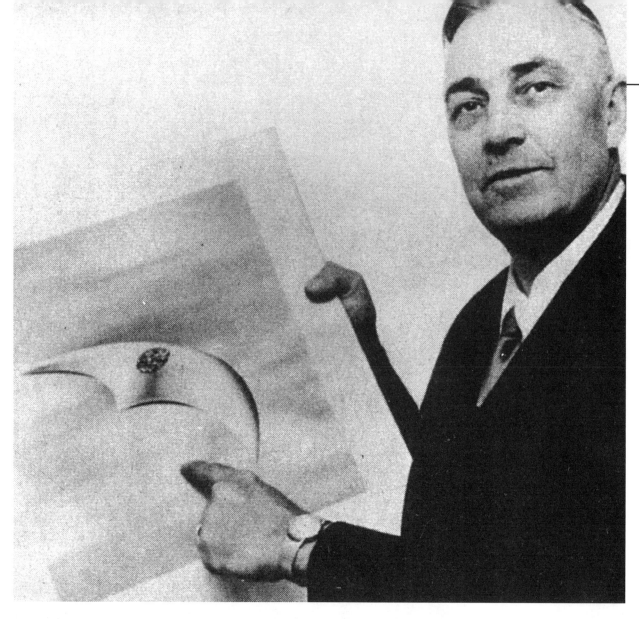

Kenneth Arnold shows an artist's impression of the crescent-shaped craft that he saw in 1947.

Arnold. He assumed that the craft were made by humans and at first thought that they were some form of top secret US military aircraft being tested. It was not until after he landed that Arnold considered that they might not be from the USA, but could be secret, high-performance Soviet intruders (this being in the early days of the Cold War). It was for this reason that Arnold reported the incident first to the FBI and then to the press. When a reporter asked Arnold to elaborate on what he meant when he said that the aircraft bobbed along he replied, 'They moved like a saucer does when you skip it over the water'. The term 'flying saucer' was born.

In hindsight, something very much more important happened that day than the mere coining of a phrase. Arnold was the first person to suggest that the strange flying objects were mechanical craft piloted by intelligent beings of unknown origin, but possibly hostile intent. The idea might seem fairly obvious to us now, but before that fateful day in 1947 other, similar objects were explained in a variety of different ways.

Something else that Arnold did, this time inadvertently, was to make it admissible for a person to report seeing a 'flying saucer', or an Unidentified Flying Object (UFO) as they soon became better known. As researchers were later to discover, these things had been seen for a great many years before 1947, but had not been recognized for what they were.

HISTORIC SIGHTINGS

Take, for instance, a report from Japan in 1361. 'An object shaped like a drum and about 20 ft [6 m] in diameter' was seen to fly low over the Inland Sea. Another Japanese report, this time from May 1606, records that a 'gigantic red wheel' hovered over Nijo Castle in Kyoto for some minutes, then began to spin and flew off.

Meanwhile other records show that odd flying objects were active in Europe. In 75BC a Roman priest recorded that: 'A spark fell from a star and grew larger as it approached the ground to become as large as the moon and as bright as the sun seen through thin clouds. On returning to the sky it took the form of a torch.'

On 5 December 1577 a number of 'flying objects shaped like hats' that were 'black, yellow and bloody' flew over Germany, and at least one of them landed temporarily. Given the style of hats at the time, the objects would seem to have been round with a low, domed shape and with a projecting edge or flange around the base.

On 15 August 1663 another odd object was seen in the skies over Robozero, Russia. It was about 11.30 am and the local peasants were gathered in the church when 'a great crash sounded from out of the heavens and many people left the church of God to assemble outside on the square. Now Levka Pedorov [a farmer who dictated this account to a local government official] was amongst them and saw what happened. To him it was a sign from God. There descended upon Robozero a great ball of fire from the clearest of skies, not from a cloud. Moreover it came from the direction from which we get winter and moved across from the church to the lake. The fire

> 'On 5 December 1577 a number of "flying objects shaped like hats" that were "black, yellow and bloody" flew over Germany, and at least one of them landed temporarily.'

was about 150 ft [45 m] on each side and for the same distance in front of the fire there were two fiery beams. Suddenly it was no longer there, but about one hour of the clock it appeared again, above the lake from which it had disappeared before. It went from the south to the west and was about 1,700 ft [500 m] away when it vanished. But once again it returned, filling all who saw it with a great dread, travelling westwards and staying over Robozero [for] one hour and a half. Now there were fishermen in the boat on the lake about a mile away and they were sorely burnt by the fire. The lake water was lit up to its greatest depths of 30 ft [9 m] and the fish fled to the banks. The water seemed to be covered with rust under the glow.'

> **'After some days of debate, the scientists came back with the answer that Yoritsume had seen the wind blowing the stars about.'**

Although the physical descriptions of many of these early reports clearly fit what we would today categorize as being UFOs, the witnesses of the time had quite different explanations. In September 1235 a Japanese nobleman named Yoritsume saw strange lights in the night sky. The lights were bright, round and moving in circling or swaying paths to the southwest. Yoritsume summoned the scientific experts of his day, described what he had seen and asked for an explanation. After some days of debate, the scientists came back with the answer that Yoritsume had seen the wind blowing the stars about.

Meanwhile in England in 793 the sight of blazing objects streaking across the daytime skies over Northumberland were recorded by the local monks as being 'dragons'.

These early reports, and there are a great many of them, clearly suggest that the UFO phenomenon has been going on for a very long time. Certainly the incidents would be classed as UFO reports if they were to happen today. Generally, however, little detail was recorded and so they cannot be used to build up much of a picture of what exactly was going on.

A DIVINE SIGHT?

Rather fuller in detail, because they were believed to be of great importance, are those incidents that the witness took to be an encounter with gods, demons or other supernatural entities.

The event that is quoted more often than any other is the meeting between the Hebrew prophet Ezekiel and God that took place on the banks of the River Chebar in 592BC. In Chapter 1 of the Book of Ezekiel in the Bible, the prophet records:

'And I looked and behold a whirlwind came out of the north, a great cloud and a fire infolding itself and a brightness was about it, and out of the midst thereof as the colour of amber out of the midst of the fire. Also out of the midst thereof came the likeness of four living creatures. And this was their appearance: they had the likeness of a man and every one had four faces and every one had four wings. And their feet were straight feet, and the sole of their feet was like the sole of a calf's foot and they sparkled like the colour of burnished brass. And they had the hands of a man under their wings on their four sides and they four had their faces and their wings. Their wings were joined one to another, they

An engraving showing the vision of Ezekiel. Some modern researchers interpret the visitation as a UFO sighting.

turned not when they went, they went every one straight forward. And their wings were stretched upward, two wings of every one were joined one to another and two covered their bodies. And they went every one straight forward, whither the spirit was to go they went and they turned not when they went. As for the likeness of the living creatures, their appearance was like burning coals of fire and like the appearance of lamps. It went up and down among the living creatures and the fire was bright and out of the fire went forth lightning.

'Behold one wheel upon the earth. The appearance of the wheels and their work was like unto the colour of a beryl and they four had one likeness and their appearance was as it were a wheel in the middle of a wheel. When they went, they went upon their four sides and they turned not when they went. As for their rings, they were so high that they were dreadful and their rings were full of eyes round about them four.

'And when they went I heard the noise of their wings like the noise of great waters, as the noise of a host.'

A modern illustration of a dragon. In medieval times odd lights in the sky might have been interpreted as fire-breathing dragons.

Ezekiel goes on to give even more detail, including what sounds like a glass dome over the wheels, before going on to explain that this bizarre and startling apparition was 'the likeness of the glory of the Lord'. He records how God had spoken to him, passing on a message of doom and catastrophe to be visited upon the Israelites for their wickedness.

Quite clearly Ezekiel was trying to describe something that he had seen which had made a massive impact upon him, but which he had not fully understood. He himself interpreted it as being a sign from God. Some modern ufologists have interpreted it as being a UFO and have sought to get behind Ezekiel's words to reconstruct exactly what it was that he saw. The work of NASA rocket designer J.F. Blumrich in producing a mechanical flying machine that matches Ezekiel's description is particularly persuasive.

It has also been pointed out that some of the appearance and behaviour of God and his angels, as recorded in the early books of the Bible, is at times distinctly ungodly.

'It has also been pointed out that some of the appearance and behaviour of God and his angels, as recorded in the early books of the Bible, is at times distinctly ungodly.'

When God and two angels visit Abraham at Mamre, as recorded in the book of Genesis, they appear as three perfectly normal – though very handsome – men. The foursome then sit down and eat a meal of roasted veal cooked by Abraham. Sitting down to a hearty meal might, some modern researchers say, be appropriate behaviour for an alien at the end of a long journey but is hardly fitting for an omnipotent deity.

Other modern writers have gone further, suggesting that most if not all early deities were, in fact, aliens. It must be admitted that the antics of many pagan deities seem to be both ungodly in their emotions and pettiness as well as very physical. It has also been pointed out that a large number of them seemed to need mechanical devices in order to carry out their divine powers. They used chariots and winged helmets to fly, and staffs or tridents to unleash destruction. All of this has been taken by

The trident of Poseidon (left), winged helmet of Mercury (centre) and chariot of Chandra (right) are curiously mechanical devices for gods to need, leading some to suppose that these pagan deities were aliens.

Brinsley le Poer Trench, known as Lord Clancarty, was a key UFO investigator during the 1960s.

Dogon, an otherwise obscure tribe of Mali in Africa, had detailed knowledge of the Sirius star system. In particular they knew that the visible star Sirius A had a much smaller star orbiting it on a cycle of 50 earth years (actually it is 50.04 years which is pretty close). They also stated that Jupiter had four moons and that the Milky Way was a vast circle of stars. They also had other astronomical knowledge, but these

> ' ... the Dogon, an otherwise obscure tribe of Mali in Africa, had detailed knowledge of the Sirius star system.'

some writers as evidence that these 'gods' were in fact very mortal beings equipped with highly advanced technology. The most obvious identification for these figures would be that they were aliens visiting Earth and should, therefore, be linked to modern reports of UFOs and their occupants.

DOGON KNOWLEDGE

The most outspoken advocates of this theory of ancient aliens have been the Swiss writer Erich von Daniken and Britain's Brinsley le Poer Trench, better known outside of paranormal circles by his title of Lord Clancarty. Both writers were most active in the 1960s and 1970s, when their ideas gained wide acceptance among many members of the public.

One of the most impressive pieces of evidence these writers put forward was the fact that the

facts were key as the stars they referred to could not be seen with the naked eye, but only with the most powerful of telescopes.

When this knowledge was collected by scientists studying Dogon customs and lifestyles in the 1930s it was considered a mysterious anomaly. The explanation given by the Dogon themselves as to how they got their knowledge was put down as being a mythological account of gods and spirits.

When the 1930s documentation was studied again, and the Dogon case re-visited in the light of more modern knowledge of UFOs and the like, the facts turned out to be rather different. The Dogon did not claim to have acquired their knowledge from the gods, but from a race of travellers who had visited the Dogon lands from a planet that orbits Sirius B. This planet, the Dogon said, was called Nyantolo, while the

A pair of Dogon tribesmen take part in a ritual dance. The Dogon claim to have been visited by aliens.

aliens who came from it were called Nommo. The Nommo are usually shown as having a long tail, rather like that of a dolphin. The Nommo had come to the Dogon territory, landing near Lake Debo, in a large flying object shaped like a round boat, that made a thundering roar as it flew.

It must be admitted that Dogon beliefs include a mass of other material that either cannot be proved to be true, or that quite clearly relates to mythological deities. But the detailed knowledge about Sirius and the explanation as to how the Dogon came by such knowledge is suggestive of ancient alien visitations. They themselves do not have any precise date for the visit by the Nommo, other than that it was a very long time ago.

Critics pointed out that some of the facts put forward by von Daniken and others to support these theories of ancient visits by aliens were not actually true. Moreover claims that von Daniken had made about first-hand visits to key sites turned out to be fictitious, when it turned out that his information had come from photos and written reports compiled by others. At the time, the revelations served to undermine the ancient alien theory and the public began to lose interest, as did those investigating modern UFO reports.

The Dogon tribe had somehow accessed highly sophisticated astronomical knowledge.

Nevertheless, these criticisms have done little to undermine the basic concept of ancient alien visits. The evidence that we currently have does indicate that there have been definite and very sudden leaps in technological knowledge and ability at certain points in human history. The ancient alien theory puts these leaps down to the benevolent intervention of visiting aliens. More conventional ideas suggest that either the sudden appearance of technology has more to do with missing evidence of a slow development or that some forgotten human genius was responsible.

DO YOU BELIEVE IN FAIRIES?

It is not only gods that have been put forward as being ancient accounts of UFO visits. The widespread belief in the various forms of fairies, elves, goblins and other assorted little people has also been linked to accounts of what we would today call UFOs and aliens. The problem here is that many 'fairy stories' have been written during the past 150 years to amuse children. These have little, if anything, to do with traditional beliefs in fairies. While the fairies of children's books are friendly and playful, the ancient fairies were powerful and capricious. While storybook fairies delight in helping humans, genuine fairies would kidnap them and subject them to unspeakable horrors.

Two typical fairy encounters could be given to make the point. In the 1860s a young woman was walking home to Kington, Herefordshire, when she saw a group of fairies dancing in a field. She went to join them, joined them in their dance for a few minutes, then left to go home. On reaching home the woman found her mother in tears and that her family and friends were all out searching for her. She had been missing for days, although she thought that only a few minutes had passed. This experience of lost time occurs again and again in encounters with UFOs and aliens.

Another encounter with fairies that reads much like a modern meeting with aliens occurred in Cornwall one evening in 1810 when a tailor named William Dunn was walking home from Truro to St Kea. He was walking down a lane near the churchyard when he was startled to see a group of small men cross the road in front of him. Each of the men was a little over 3 ft (1 m) tall and dressed in red with an oddly shaped hat or helmet. The figures walked in single

> **'The figures walked in single file across the road, scrambled over the hedge and walked off across a field. Dunn tried to follow them, but found that his arms and legs were paralyzed.'**

file across the road, scrambled over the hedge and walked off across a field. Dunn tried to follow them, but found that his arms and legs were paralyzed. He watched as the procession vanished into a mound. For a few minutes Dunn could not move, but then suddenly regained the use of his limbs. He believed the figures to have been 'piskies' and that he had been charmed into immobility. The description he gave of his piskies would match that of many modern aliens, while temporary paralysis has been reported by many witnesses to UFO activity.

AIRSHIPS AND INDUSTRY

Moving on from the admittedly ambiguous or imprecise accounts from the distant past, there is a mass of reports dating to before 1947 that is consistent with the UFO phenomenon. These reports have often been made by educated people, familiar with the mechanical technology of the industrial revolution. While they have

A Victorian painting of a troupe of fairies, supernatural beings that share many similarities with the descriptions of humanoids that emerge from UFOs.

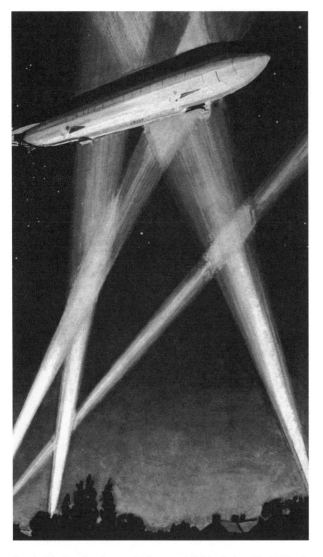

An airship bomber is caught in searchlights during World War I.

airships were the only large flying craft produced by humans. They could be up to 300 ft (90 m) long at a time when aeroplanes were fragile canvas and wood affairs just a few metres long. It was, perhaps, natural for a witness of the time to assume that anything big and airborne was an airship.

At 7 pm on 17 November 1896 a large cigar-shaped object that emitted a bright white light glided over a suburb of Sacramento, California. One of the many witnesses to the craft thought that he heard a voice call down 'We hope to be in San Francisco by tomorrow noon'. That would have been good going for a contemporary airship.

On 25 January 1897 another 'airship' was seen over Hastings, Nebraska. This craft was in sight for over 30 minutes as it hovered, circled and cruised about. The object was equipped with a bright light that swept around in circles, illuminating the ground below. In April that year a broadly similar craft was seen manoeuvring over Brown County, Kansas.

On 23 April the series of sightings went up a gear when Judge Lawrence Byrne of Arkansas encountered not only an airship, but also its crew. He said that the occupants of the craft 'looked like Japs' and spoke a language he could not understand. Presumably the judge meant that the occupants were small, yellowish and had slanting eyes, since that was the typical view of Japanese people in the Midwest at the time.

During August reports came in from Vancouver, British Columbia and parts of northern Mexico as well

not interpreted what they saw as being a UFO or related to aliens, their descriptions are much clearer and more precise than the older reports coloured by belief in pagan gods or fairies.

Between 1895 and 1914 there came a series of reports of mysterious flying objects, some of them with a humanoid crew, that were at the time believed to be airships of some advanced design. At this date as several locations in the USA. By October the number of sightings declined and by January 1898 the mysterious craft had vanished.

At the time the most popular theory to account for these sightings was that a rich and very clever American scientist had developed a revolutionary new type of airship and was carrying out trials. When the sightings petered out and no such inventor came forward with his device, the idea was dropped. The sightings were quietly forgotten until later UFO researchers turned them up.

Meanwhile the trail of airship sightings moved to New Zealand. On 23 July 1909 an airship dived down from the clouds to hover over a school at Kelso on South Island. It was seen by dozens of children and all the teachers as it hovered overhead for 10 minutes before climbing back up into the cloud cover.

Three days later an airship as big as a house was seen floating over Kaka Point on South Island. The airship appeared just after dusk and seemed to be illuminated from within. After circling for a while it flew off.

'BRITAIN INVADED'

That same year the airships appeared over Britain. At this date tensions with Germany were high and many people expected Germany to launch a pre-emptive invasion of Britain. It was known that Germany had several gigantic airships, manufactured by Count Zeppelin, that were able to fly from Germany to Britain

carrying bombs, and it was predicted that any German invasion would be preceded by Zeppelin bombing attacks.

'... the First Lord of the Admiralty, one Winston Churchill, had to admit that the government did not know what the mysterious craft might be.'

When what looked like a Zeppelin cruised over the coastal town of Southend on 20 May 1909, many residents feared the worst. The local newspaper next day carried the headline 'Britain Invaded'. The aerial intruder was described as being a 'mysterious cigar-shaped machine with quivering lights and whirring mechanisms'. Over the following days identical aircraft were spotted over Norwich, Birmingham and the Welsh town of Pontypool.

The airships then left Britain, but returned in greater numbers three years later. Between November 1912 and January 1913 dozens of sightings of Zeppelin-like airships took place at Cardiff, Liverpool, Dover and other cities. The matter reached the House of Commons where the First Lord of the Admiralty, one Winston Churchill, had to admit that the government did not know what the mysterious craft might be.

In 1942 a new class of mysterious flying objects appeared in the war-torn skies over Europe. These

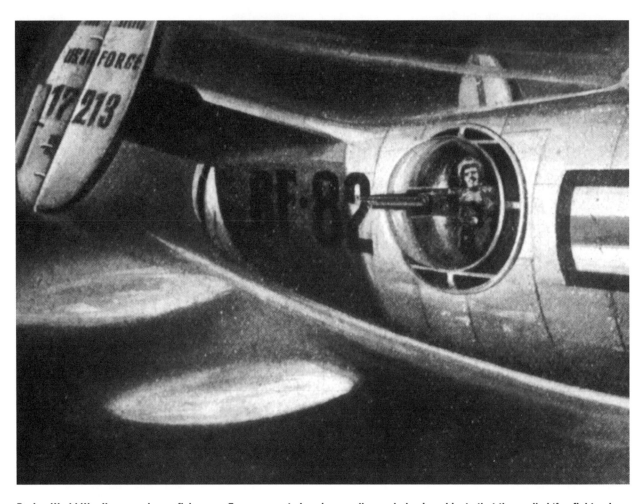

During World War II, many airmen flying over Europe reported seeing small, round glowing objects that they called 'foo fighters'.

became known to British and American airmen as 'foo fighters'. These objects were typically fairly small, less than 10 ft (3 m) across, and were spherical or disc-shaped. At night the foo fighters glowed with an eerie light, but during the day seemed to be made of aluminium. They habitually flew alongside aircraft, but sometimes hovered still in the path of an aircraft.

The aircrews were, understandably, nervous that these strange objects were some German secret weapon. At first it was feared that they were weapons packed with explosives, but when none was ever seen to explode, the idea that they were surveillance craft gained favour. After the war the Allied intelligence staff diligently searched the German files and interrogated German scientists, but it turned out that the Germans had been as mystified by the objects as were the Allies. Indeed Luftwaffe pilots had been just as wary of the foo fighters as had their opponents.

In 1946 sightings of strange rockets took place across Scandinavia. The craft were usually described as being wingless, streamlined and of a silver colour. They were estimated to fly at over 1,000 mph (1,600 kmph) and sometimes they trailed smoke or flames, but often they did not. The authorities jumped to the conclusion that these craft were an advanced form of the terrible V2 rocket that had been used by the Germans to devastating effect on London, Rotterdam and other cities during the raids of 1944 and 1945.

The chief suspect was the Soviet Union. When Swedish officials demanded answers, the Soviets denied all knowledge of the 'ghost rockets'. They pointed out that if they were testing new weapons they would be more likely to do so over Siberia than over Sweden. Nevertheless, fears that a foreign power was testing weapons remained. Swedish newspapers were banned from printing the location of sightings, while the Norwegian government imposed a total news blackout. Nevertheless reports continued to be made for many months and did not cease until the early 1950s.

Although there were an impressive number of unexplained flying objects being seen around the world, the subject had never been given much weight in the media. Nor, it would seem, had official authorities linked up the various groups of sightings as being different aspects of the one phenomenon. Each rash of sightings remained a purely local sensation that was not taken up by the international media. The stories may have got plenty of coverage in local or regional press, but that was all.

It was Kenneth Arnold's sighting that really got the world interested in UFOs. As can be seen, Arnold's sighting was neither spectacular nor especially bizarre. Compared to some earlier and later sightings it was decidedly run-of-the-mill. What marked it out were the links to possible Soviet high-tech weaponry over the USA, Arnold's unimpeachable honesty and the coining of the term 'flying saucer'.

Once the idea of flying saucers had been exposed and discussed in the American press and across radio networks, it spread rapidly to other nations in the developed world. At first only those nations with links to the USA took up the story – Britain, Australia, Canada, the nations of western Europe and so on. The media in the Communist Bloc and the Third World did not carry the stories – which is not to say that sightings did not take place in those countries.

GATHERING MOMENTUM

Within three months of Arnold's sighting hitting the headlines, over 800 reports of strange aerial objects had been made to the US Air Force. In the months that followed the number of reports declined, but they continued to be made, often by highly reputable witnesses in clear conditions – though there were inevitably some reports of events that took place in poor visibility or that were made by people whose veracity might, for one reason or another, be suspect.

An early note of humour was injected into the growing story by the events of 4 July 1947. The news of Arnold's sighting barely two weeks earlier was spreading quickly through aviation circles, leading to intense speculation. That lunchtime a discussion among airline staff at Boise Airport was cut short by United Airlines pilot E.J. Smith, who declared flatly that it was all nonsense. 'I'll believe them when I see them,' he finished, slamming down his newspaper and striding off to get his aircraft ready for flight.

Smith took off and barely 20 minutes later found himself confronted by five disc-shaped flying objects, each of which was larger than his own DC3 airliner. The objects were also seen by the co-pilot and stewardess before they flew off at high speed.

Typical of the early reports that attracted official notice was that made by Eastern Airlines pilots Clarence Chiles and John Whitted. On the night of 23 July 1948 they were flying a DC3 passenger flight over Alabama when they sighted what they took to be another aircraft some distance ahead of them. Within seconds Chiles and Whitted realized that the other aircraft was coming towards them at great speed. They braced themselves to take emergency evasive action to avoid a collision, but the object passed them at a distance of a few hundred feet, then shot away to vanish into the distance behind them.

The mystery aircraft had been in sight for only a few seconds, but had come very close and both men were confident that they had got a good look at it. They reported that the object was shaped like a rocket or cigar and that it glowed pale blue over its entire surface with a brightness that hurt their eyes when it was at its closest. There was a row of what might have been windows along the centre of the craft's side. There were small flames or fumes coming from the rear of the object. Whitted later described what he had seen as 'a Flash Gordon rocket ship'.

> **'Smith took off and barely 20 minutes later found himself confronted by five disc-shaped flying objects, each of which was larger than his own DC3 airliner.'**

SKY-FIGHT

On 1 October 1948 one of the most famous and best documented of the early sightings took place. At 9 pm, 26-year-old Lieutenant George Gorman of the Air National Guard was on a routine practice flight in an F51 fighter. He was at an altitude of about 4,500 ft (1,400 m) and approaching Fargo Airport to land when he spotted a light moving below him.

Gorman thought that he was looking at the tail light of another aircraft, and estimated it to be about 3,500 ft (1,000 m) beneath him and flying on a roughly parallel course at around 250 mph (400 kmph). Worried that another aircraft was on his landing flight path, Gorman called up the Fargo air traffic control, manned by L.D. Jensen. Jensen replied

United Airlines pilot E.J. Smith shows a stewardess how the UFO he saw in 1947 had behaved in flight.

that the only other aircraft in the area was a Piper Cub a safe distance to the west. Gorman looked, and located the Cub. Looking back at the mystery light, Gorman watched as it flew over a floodlit football ground and was astonished to see that it was not attached to an aircraft but was a flying globe of light.

Alerted by Gorman, Jensen contacted Manuel Johnson in the control tower. Johnson got out his binoculars and located the light, confirming that it was not attached to an aircraft. Jensen peered into the sky, and he too saw the odd light. So too, once alerted by radio to the unfolding drama, did Dr A. Cannon and Einar Nelson in the Cub.

When the mystery light turned and began a dive toward the airport, Gorman decided to act. He was, after all, in the National Guard and flying in a fighter aircraft. He decided to give chase. Gorman later related 'I dived after it at full speed [about 400 mph or 650 kmph in an F51] but I couldn't catch the thing. I put my 51 into a sharp turn and tried to cut it off. By then we were at about 7,000 ft (2,100 m). Suddenly it made a sharp right turn and we headed straight at each other. Just when we were about to collide I guess I lost my nerve. I went into a dive and the light passed over my canopy. Then it made a left circle about 1,000 ft (300 m) above and I gave chase again.'

This time, Gorman decided, he would not pull out of any collision. Indeed he was quite prepared to ram the mystery object and radioed his intention to Fargo. Jensen and Johnson had by now abandoned their tasks and were able to follow the extraordinary dogfight that followed. For some 20 minutes Gorman and the mystery light chased each other around the sky over Fargo. Then the intruder seemed to tire of the proceedings. The light began a steep climb. Gorman followed it up to 17,000 ft (5,200 m), but was unable to keep up. The object flew off to the northwest at high speed. Gorman landed and filed a report.

Unfortunately for Gorman, word got out about his intention to ram the mysterious flying object. Several newspapers speculated that the USAF had issued their pilots with orders to ram flying saucers if they got the chance, rather than to shoot them down. In fact no such order existed and at first the Air Force thought Gorman had made the statement and considered court-martialling him. The idea was dropped when it became clear that it was merely journalists speculating.

HOT AIR

The Gorman dogfight had a number of portents for the future. One of the most notable has largely been missed by many later researchers. When investigators from the USAF came to research the incident and seek an explanation, they questioned Gorman closely and in detail for some hours. They checked to see if any other aircraft had been in the area, they looked for reports of meteors or the like. They drew a complete blank. That was when they suggested to Gorman that what he had seen was a weather balloon.

The weather balloons of the time carried a small light so that they could be tracked by the weather observers. It was suggested that Gorman, tired after his long training flight, had misidentified the object, and had confused its movements relative to the fast moving F51 fighter with real movements. Gorman told them he was sure it was not a balloon and that he was absolutely certain that the light had been moving, and at speed. Clearly the USAF investigators were unimpressed and wanted to put the event down as a misidentified weather balloon. 'They had it just about wrapped up,' Gorman said later.

But the Fargo weather observer, George Sanderson, had been keeping meticulous records. He confirmed that no weather balloons had been in the air at the

A US military weather balloon of the type that the USAF repeatedly claimed to be the cause of UFO sightings.

time. The investigators put the events down as officially 'unexplained'.

Nevertheless a magazine article that appeared on 7 May 1949, and included details that seemed to have come from the official documentation, concluded that Gorman had been chasing a weather balloon. Not a weather balloon from Fargo, but a military high altitude helium balloon launched from Minneapolis. The article speculated that such a balloon launched a few hours earlier had leaked gas and lost altitude so that it was drifting over Fargo at the time Gorman was coming into land. How a leaking balloon could leave by climbing rapidly was not explained.

At the time several independent researchers thought that the helium balloon story had been placed by the USAF in the magazine to try to kill the

Gorman story. The first attempt by the USAF to blame an ordinary weather balloon had failed, so now they turned to a different sort of balloon as a supposed explanation. It was a suspected ploy by the military that would have echoes many years later in a much more famous case.

UP A GEAR

Another similar encounter took place on 4 December 1952 over Laredo in Texas. A regular USAF officer, named at the time as Earl Fogle although this was probably a pseudonym, was on a night patrol in the direction of the Mexican border when he saw a blue, round object flying some distance away. The object had changed direction to intercept Fogle's F51 fighter. It then turned on to a collision course and approached at high speed. At the last moment the object turned aside, climbed steeply then came down for a second pass. This being peacetime, Fogle had been flying with his lights on. He now turned them off and dived rapidly away from the approaching object. Glancing over his shoulder, Fogle saw the blue object circle as if looking for him, then it climbed away and vanished from sight.

Thus far only fairly low-performance propeller aircraft had encountered flying saucers in the air. It was soon to be the turn of high-performance jet fighters and the USAF airmen were in for a shock.

On 29 October 1952 two of the latest model F94 jet fighters were patrolling off Long Island. The F94 was

The astronomer Clyde Tombaugh sights eight mysterious green lights in the sky over his house in the Arizona desert in 1949.

not only heavily armed and fast, but had air-to-air radar operated by a second crew member sitting behind the pilot. The two aircraft were piloted by Lieutenant Burt Deane and Lieutenant Ralph Corbett. At about 2 am Deane saw a bright white light ahead of the jets at an estimated 8 miles (13 km) distance.

Aware that they were the first fast fighters to get this close to a flying saucer, Deane and Corbett decided to attack. Corbett got a radar lock first, but it was Deane who pushed his fighter to full power to close in for the attack. At once the UFO began to move quickly, cutting inside the curve of Deane's turn. Deane pulled his fighter into its tightest possible turn, almost blacking out due to the extreme g-force, but he could not match the performance of the mystery aircraft. Corbett now came up to the attack, using standard fighter tactics to try to push the UFO into range of Deane's guns. It was to no avail. Whatever the pilots tried, the UFO managed to slip aside at the last moment — often at speeds or performing turns quite impossible for the pursuing F94 fighters. After about 10 minutes of dogfighting, the UFO climbed steeply away at supersonic speed. Deane and Corbett gave chase but were rapidly outpaced.

In the report he filed after landing, Deane wrote 'Based on my experience of fighter tactics, it is my opinion that the object was controlled by something having visual contact with us. The power and acceleration were beyond the capability of any known USAF aircraft.' The investigators who questioned the two pilots about the incident again put it down as 'unexplained'.

'Deane pulled his fighter into its tightest possible turn, almost blacking out due to the extreme g-force'

It was not only military airmen who were encountering flying saucers. On 20 August 1949 no less a figure than Clyde Tombaugh, the astronomer who had discovered Pluto, got involved in the growing mystery of flying saucers. At 10.45 pm he was sitting outside his house at Las Cruces, New Mexico, with his wife and her mother. His eye was caught by a green light flying overhead. Looking up, Tombaugh saw seven other lights, all of the same green colour and all flying a parallel course. He thought that he could just make out a dark shape behind the lights, as if they were windows or lights attached to a large, unlit aircraft, but he could not be certain. The craft made no sound as it powered overhead and vanished into the distance.

On 20 May the following year another astronomer saw a flying saucer. This was Dr Seymour Hess of the Lowell Observatory at Flagstaff, Arizona. He was outside the observatory checking cloud cover when he spotted a bright object in the sky. He studied it through his binoculars for some seconds as it flew past. The object was a shiny disc that was flying through thin cloud, sometimes disappearing behind

Clyde Tombaugh, the astronomer who discovered Pluto, poses by his homemade telescope in Las Cruces in 1987.

the cloud and at other times flying beneath it. After a few seconds the object flew out of sight.

Not far away, at Farmington, New Mexico, the afternoon of 18 March proved to be an historic one for flying saucer investigators. For well over half an hour, the skies over the small town were filled with dozens of disc-shaped aircraft flying in formation, performing manoeuvres, diving, climbing and swooping. One witness among the hundreds who saw the event described it as 'A fantastic air circus'. Even the local sheriff watched, unable to explain events.

KEY RESEARCH

One man who was determined to explain was retired US Marines officer Major Donald Keyhoe. Keyhoe was a respected writer on aviation matters who in May 1949 was hired by Ken Purdy, editor of *True Magazine,* to investigate the flying saucer stories and write an article. Keyhoe's life was to be changed forever. He devoted the rest of his life to the study of the UFO phenomenon, producing several respected books. He was to die in 1988.

At the time, Purdy was of the view that the flying

saucer reports had been invented by the USAF as a cover story for some secret project. Keyhoe was equally dismissive. With his knowledge of aviation matters he knew that the speeds and appearances of the flying saucers being reported were simply impossible for the technology of the time. Keyhoe did consider it an outside possibility that the reports might refer to a top secret British missile that he had heard was being tested by the RAF, but did not think that that weapon had the capabilities – and as things transpired it did not.

For some weeks Keyhoe worked on the assumption that either the objects were being misreported or that the USAF was testing some secret weapon and was itself behind the flying saucer reports to cover up the truth. Gradually, however, Keyhoe came to believe that the USAF was trying to discredit and cover up the flying saucer reports, not disseminate them.

In 1950 Keyhoe reviewed the evidence that he had uncovered, both of the reality of flying saucers and of attempts by the USAF to cover it up. He came to several conclusions. The first was that the reports of flying saucers by and large accurately related the existence of large flying machines of unknown origin capable of extraordinary speeds and manoeuvres. Second, he believed that the USAF high command knew exactly what the flying saucers were and where they came from, but were desperate to hide this truth from the American public. Third, he decided that the

only explanation to fit the facts was that the flying saucers were alien spacecraft carrying highly intelligent beings from another planet.

Keyhoe speculated that the reason why there had been a massive upsurge in flying saucer reports, and so in the number of alien visits, since 1947, was to be found in recent events. He held that the explosion of the first atomic bombs in 1945 marked some kind of a threshold in the technological development of a civilization. The time lag of two years from the atomic blasts of 1945 and the upsurge in alien visits in 1947

> **'Gradually, ... Keyhoe came to believe that the USAF was trying to discredit and cover up the flying saucer reports, not disseminate them.'**

had been the time taken for the distant alien civilization to detect the atomic bomb explosions and to respond.

In 1950 he published his classic book *The Flying Saucers are Real.* In this book he detailed his investigations and propounded his theories. The book was massively popular, selling half a million copies within weeks. It established the basic beliefs of the early years of UFO study and its central message remains important to this day.

Meanwhile the reports of flying saucers continued to come in.

KENT SIGHTING

In 1953 the flying saucer wave crossed the Atlantic when the West Malling Incident took place. On 3 November two RAF officers, T. S. Johnson and G. Smythe, were flying a reconnaissance mission in their Vampire jet fighter. They were at 20,000 ft (6,000 m) over West Malling in Kent when they spotted a round, brightly lit object high above them.

As the two airmen watched, the strange object dived toward their fighter. As it drew closer they saw that it was disc-shaped and that a ring of intensely bright lights glared out from its rim. The object flew around the Vampire, then made off at high speed. It had been in sight for about 30 seconds. Meanwhile the object had been picked up by a radar station at Lee Green, also in Kent, and had been seen from the ground by a member of the anti-aircraft gun crew at RAF West Malling.

News of the sighting leaked to the local newspapers, and was taken up by the national media. Three weeks after the event one of Kent's Members of Parliament, Colonel Schofield, asked a question in the House of Commons about the incident. The Minister of Defence at the time, Mr Birch, replied 'Two experimental meteorological balloons were observed at different times on 3 November. There was nothing peculiar about either of the occurrences.' Another MP, Mr Isaacs, jumped up to ask a supplementary question: 'Will the Minister agree that this story of flying saucers is all

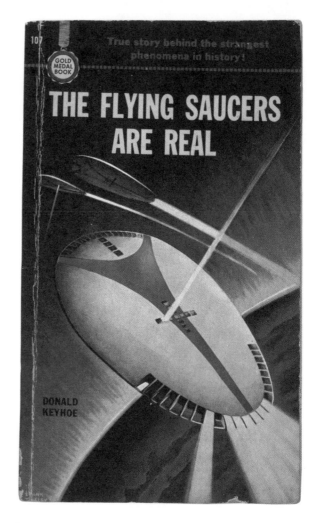

The cover to the book by Donald Keyhoe which first put forward the idea that UFOs were alien spacecraft.

ballooney?' The house dissolved in laughter, then moved on to other business.

Many suspected that Mr Isaacs had been fed his witty question in advance by the government to detract attention from the incident. If so, it worked. As in the Gorman dogfight sighting in America, the authorities used weather balloons as an unlikely explanation of a very serious event.

It was about this date that strange rumours began to spread among newspapermen and others investigating the mysterious objects. It was reported that one, two or more of the flying saucers had crashed somewhere in the southwestern USA. The wreckage had, it was said, been impounded by the US Air Force and a tight blanket of secrecy imposed on the whole affair.

On 22 March the story came to the attention of the FBI when Guy Hottel, an officer in Washington DC, sent in a report based on a conversation with a senior USAF officer. The report runs: 'An investigator for the Air Force stated that three so-called flying saucers had been recovered in New Mexico. They were described as being circular in shape with raised centres, approximately 50 ft (15 m) in diameter. Each one was occupied by three bodies of human shape, but only 3 ft (1 m) tall, dressed in metallic cloth of a very fine texture. The saucers were found in New Mexico due to the fact that the government has a very high-powered radar set-up in that area and it is believed the radar interferes with the controlling mechanism of the saucers.' The FBI took no action on the report. Perhaps the senior officials thought it was all nonsense – or perhaps they knew something of what lay behind the report and did not need to follow it up.

As the story developed it had, by 1950, assumed a definitive form. Two saucers had crashed somewhere in Arizona or New Mexico. Inside the craft had been found the dead bodies of several humanoids each about 3 ft (1 m) tall. The creatures were undamaged and did not appear to have been killed by the forces of impact, fire or other causes normal to an air crash. The figures had all been dressed identically in what seemed to be a uniform of some kind. The speculation was that the craft had come down by accident, and the crews then died as a result of

'It was generally speculated that the "little men from Venus" had died as the result of an infection or due to an inability to breath Earth's atmosphere.'

some natural contamination. It was generally speculated that the 'little men from Venus' had died as the result of an infection or due to an inability to breath Earth's atmosphere. The US Air Force, it was said, had hushed the story up so that they could educate the public gradually to the existence of extraterrestrials visiting Earth.

The story was not, as a rule, taken very seriously. Donald Keyhoe declared that 'The story has all the earmarks of a well-thought-out hoax' and refused to spend time looking into it.

As we shall see later in this book, the story might have actually had more to it than Keyhoe and others at the time believed.

CHAPTER 2

ARMED RECONNAISSANCE

Fort Knox, the fortified home of the US gold reserves, was the focus for a fatal UFO encounter in 1948.

At 2.15 pm on 7 January 1948 a Virginia State Police patrol on the highway near Madisonville radioed an urgent alarm to their base. A large, disc-shaped object gleaming silver and red had flashed overhead at low level. And it was heading for the main US gold reserve store at Fort Knox. According to the police report, dozens of people in Madisonville had seen the object pass by.

The police immediately alerted the guards on duty at Fort Knox. At this date nobody knew what to make of the flying saucers, with some people thinking that they might be top secret Soviet attack aircraft. That such a craft – whatever it was – was heading for the most vital part of the US government financial system was deeply alarming. Fort Knox alerted the USAF base at Godman Air Field, which provided air cover to the gold storehouse.

At Godman, three P51 fighters were already in the air on a routine flight to Standiford Air Field. They were contacted, briefed, and went roaring off toward Fort Knox. But the flying saucer had changed direction and appeared over Godman at 2.40 pm while the fighters were over Fort Knox.

Colonel Guy Hix, the Commanding Officer of Godman, was in the control tower when the object arrived. There was broken cloud, but the large, round object had been unmistakable as it flew south of the base. The chief executive officer, Woods, managed to get a brief fix on it and estimated it to be about 140 ft (43 m) long. A radio message was instantly sent to the fighters ordering them to return to Godman and give chase.

The flight commander was Captain Thomas Mantell, an experienced pilot of the propeller-driven P51 fighter. As he and his comrades approached Godman he

An artist's impression of the last moments of USAF pilot Thomas Mantell as his fighter is shot down by a UFO.

radioed: 'I've sighted the thing. It looks metallic and it's tremendous in size.' A few seconds later he added, 'It's starting to climb. It's at 12 o'clock [straight ahead of him] and making half my speed. I'll try to close in.'

A few minutes later Mantell reported that the mystery intruder had accelerated to 360 mph (580 kmph). Then his wingman reported that he and his comrade were abandoning the chase, while Mantell raced on ahead. At 3.15 pm Mantell's voice came on the radio again. 'It is still above me, making my speed

or better. I'm going up to 20,000 ft (6,000 m). If I'm no closer, I'll abandon the chase.'

Mantell's aircraft was not fitted with oxygen for high altitude flying, so the decision to abandon the chase at 20,000 ft was wise, even though the P51 was able to reach 41,000 ft (12,500 m).

Back in Godman control tower, Hix, Woods and others waited anxiously. When no further message came from Mantell, they tried calling him. There was no answer. The two wingmen turned their aircraft back toward the last reported position of the UFO, but could see nothing. Search aircraft were sent out and the wreckage of Mantell's aircraft was spotted. Mantell was dead. His aircraft had broken up in mid-air and been shattered into a thousand pieces that fell over a wide area, indicating that the break-up had occurred at high altitude.

Two hours later a UFO that looked very much like the one that Mantell had been chasing was spotted flying fast and low over Columbus, Ohio.

For months the USAF refused to comment officially on the death of Mantell or the UFO that he had been chasing. Then off-the-record briefings were made to a few selected aeronautical journalists. These stated that Mantell had been chasing the planet Venus, and that he had blacked out when his aircraft flew above 25,000 ft (7,600 m). The aircraft, the tale went, had continued its climb up to around 30,000 ft (9,150 m), then with no one controlling it, had gone into a steep dive with the engine on full power. The stresses of this power dive had caused the aircraft to break up at around 15,000 ft (4,500 m). This version soon became the accepted official explanation.

Mantell would have been neither the first nor the last pilot to mistake Venus for an aircraft. The planet can shine very brightly, and in some atmospheric conditions it appears to be abnormally large. During World War II several air gunners had opened fire on Venus, mistaking it for an approaching enemy nightfighter. But such mistakes had only ever been momentary, the percipient rapidly realizing his mistake. And yet Mantell had been chasing the UFO, or Venus, for over 20 minutes.

The small, but growing band of flying saucer researchers were contemptuous of the USAF explanation. Not only had Mantell been a highly experienced pilot, but Venus had not even been in the part of the sky where he reported the saucer to be. What's more, a stationary Venus could not possibly explain the moving silver and red object reported by those on the ground.

'The small, but growing band of flying saucer researchers were contemptuous of the USAF explanation.'

In December 1949 the USAF changed its story, this time issuing an official report. Now the explanation was that Mantell had died in a similar way to the previous story, blacking out at altitude, but now he was said to have been chasing not Venus but a US Navy high altitude research balloon. As in the Gorman and West Malling cases, it was a weather balloon that was being used to explain away the inexplicable.

Incredibly, this new explanation was accepted not only by the general press, but by the vast majority of saucer researchers. Only Donald Keyhoe, who early in his career had worked with weather balloons, refused to give it credence. He pointed out that the

> **'... the fact remains that Mantell set off to pursue a flying saucer that had been seen by dozens of witnesses, many of them highly trustworthy ...'**

movements reported for the object were completely inconsistent with it being a balloon. And the object had vanished less than ten minutes after Mantell's death, although there was very little wind to blow a balloon away. Some years later, Keyhoe managed to get access to the records of all civilian and military high altitude balloon releases that took place on the day Mantell died, and the few days beforehand. There were none in the area.

And yet, Mantell's death rapidly fell out of the headlines. Even among those who research UFOs it is today widely ignored. It is astonishing that the death of an experienced USAF fighter pilot engaged in the chase of a large and well-attested UFO should have been ignored as it has.

The death of Mantell provides direct evidence that whatever the saucers may be, and whoever may control them, their primary purpose is not to be benevolent to humanity. The saucer may not have attacked Mantell's aircraft – it may have responded to an aggressive move by Mantell. But the fact remains that Mantell set off to pursue a flying saucer that had been seen by dozens of witnesses, many of them highly trustworthy, and that he had ended up dead.

Some would see the Mantell Incident as an example of how effectively the authorities can cover up even the most dramatic of incidents when they really want to do so. As we shall see in a later chapter, it was soon after this that the US Government decided its best policy was to 'explain away' saucer sightings. The reasons for that decision remain controversial.

Meanwhile, sightings of saucers continued to occur. For those seeking to understand what the saucers were and why they were appearing, the behaviour described in these reports would prove to be crucial.

HEAD-ON IMPACT

In fact Mantell was not the only USAF pilot to be killed when chasing a UFO. On 23 November 1953, just after dark, a military radar picked up an unidentified aircraft behaving in an odd way over Lake Michigan, near Soo Locks. An F89C Scorpion fighter piloted by Lieutenant Felix Moncla and with Lieutenant R. Wilson as navigator was scrambled to intercept.

The radar operator monitored the progress of the jet and of the mystery craft. He vectored the jet in towards the intruder and advised Moncla when the object, if it were a normal aircraft with lights, should be within sight. He received a routine acknowledgement. Suddenly the unidentified craft changed direction and headed straight at the jet. The two signals merged, remained stationary for a few seconds and then faded.

The Moon (left) and Venus (right). When low in the sky, Venus can appear to move as air currents disrupt the view.

Fearing that a collision had taken place, the radar operator alerted the coastguard and a full-scale search and rescue mission was mounted. Nothing was found. Nothing has been found ever since. The event remains a mystery.

Most sightings were, however, non fatal. On 14 October 1954 Flight Lieutenant Salandin of the RAF's NO.604 Squadron was flying a Meteor jet fighter over Kent when he saw three round flying objects high above him. Two of the objects made off, but the third dived down towards him. It came to within 200 yds (183 m) of Salandin who later described it as being 'saucer shaped with a bun on top and a bun below, and it was silvery and metallic. There were no portholes, flames or anything.' After passing the Meteor, the object climbed away out of sight at high speed.

The epidemic of flying saucer reports was spreading rapidly, leading many researchers to recognize by the early 1950s that the phenomenon was a global one. Or at least it was among the more economically advanced parts of the world, as yet no reports had come in from developing countries.

AUSTRALIAN SIGHTINGS

On 3 May 1952 a UFO was seen flying over Wollongong in New South Wales, Australia, at 6 am. Among the couple of dozen people who were up early enough to see it was a civilian airline pilot who described the object as being shaped like a submarine, about 150 ft (46 m) long and with a pair of bright lights at either end. He thought it was flying at about 500 mph (805 kmph).

A week later the residents of Parramatta, also in New South Wales, saw a large silver globe with what appeared to be a halo of light glowing around it, flying slowly overhead.

The following year the Australian sightings moved to Victoria. At 10 pm on 3 January, the staff of a radio station in Geelong were leaving work when they spotted a bright yellow disc flying overhead. The object was moving slowly, leaving behind a trail of glowing mist. Suddenly it took off at high speed and vanished from sight.

Later that month another airline pilot, Douglas Barker, saw an object that he said was shaped rather

The entrance sign to the USAF air base that was the site of an early radar-visual UFO sighting in 1957.

like a mushroom but made of shiny metal, flying over the Yarra Valley. 'It was moving in and out of cloud at about 2,000 ft (610 m)', he reported, 'and travelling faster than any jet I have seen.' Something similar, but trailing a shower of orange sparks, flew over the town of Moorabin and was seen by local resident Mrs Banner.

In the more remote northern areas of Australia things were slower to get going. It was, in fact, at Port Moresby in Papua New Guinea that the first reliable northern sighting took place. Mr T. Drury, a former RAF officer currently serving at the civilian airport saw an odd object that he thought looked rather like a silver missile flying over the town. Fortunately he had a cine camera to hand, so he was able to snatch a few seconds of footage before the object flew out of sight.

Drury sent the film to the Australian Air Ministry, which passed it on to the USAF for expert analysis. The USAF not only refused to release their findings, they did not send the film back to him either. Fortunately Drury had made a copy before sending it out, which he then had subjected to independent analysis. It was found to show a solid object of a reflective silvery colour that was shaped like an elongated cigar. The object moved horizontally, relative to clouds in the frame, then turned a sharp right angle corner before moving upward until it vanished from sight, leaving a vapour trail as it reached high altitude. Due to the lack of any other solid objects in the frame, it was not possible to deduce the size or speed of the object from the footage alone.

RADAR-VISUAL ENCOUNTER

In 1957 what seemed to be an important new breakthrough took place. Until this date UFOs had been detected only with the human eye or caught on inconclusive film. But on 4 November 1957 what became known as a 'radar-visual' encounter took place over New Mexico.

Two control tower operators at Kirtland USAF airfield noticed a strange flying object some distance away. Tracking it through binoculars the men saw that it was metallic in composition, but lacked wings,

> **'Radar ... is no more able to explain away the UFOs as mundane objects than human observers have been.'**

blades or engines of any noticeable kind. It was of a roughly oval or rectangular shape and was positioned lengthways in the air. One of the men thought to phone the airfield's radar operator to see if he could get a lock on the object. He could, and for the next three or four minutes the object was tracked both visually and on radar. Both detected the same movements of the object at the same time, so it was evident that they were following the same thing.

The Kirtland case, and other radar-visual encounters that have taken place, do not prove what UFOs actually are. What they do establish is that the UFOs are real objects. If they were hallucinations or misidentified stars or meteors, they would not show up on radar. And if they were normal aircraft seen under unusual circumstances, as some have maintained, then the radar would have revealed them for what they were. But radar has not: it is no more able to explain away the UFOs as mundane objects than human observers have been.

Hundreds of other reports of unusual and unidentifiable flying objects poured in throughout the 1950s and beyond. Gradually a picture began to emerge of what the things looked like. Although some individual reports broke the trend, the vast majority fitted into a standard pattern.

The typical 'flying saucer', or 'UFO' as the mysterious objects were becoming known, was between 30 and 100 ft (9–30 m) in size. When seen during the day the objects seemed to be made of highly reflective silver or grey metal. The surface of the objects was free of anything that might indicate welding or rivetting, and appeared to be completely smooth and seamless. Sometimes windows were seen, and occasionally a transparent dome topped the object. At other times the dome was of the same metallic material as the rest of the object. At night the objects glowed or pulsated with a variety of colours, often changing shades and hues with a pulsating rhythm. They sometimes shone forth beams of bright light. UFOs frequently disrupted electrical equipment, especially radios. It was as if they emitted a strong electrical or magnetic field.

None of this gave very much of a clue as to what the flying saucers, or the beings who were presumed to travel in them or control them, were up to. The UFOs usually seemed to be travelling from one place to another. Where they had come from, where they were going and why could not be deduced from either their appearance or manoeuvres.

TOUCHING DOWN

Of the reports that the saucers had landed, one of the very first to be investigated and treated with some seriousness came from Australia in 1953. On 21 January Alan and Arnold Schnitzerling were driving their truck home to their farm near Graceville in Queensland. They suddenly noticed that the truck was being followed by a round, globular object that glowed a bright white, fading to a dull red.

Due to the poor road surface, the Schnitzerling brothers were driving at a speed of about 20 mph (32 kmph), and the object had no trouble keeping pace with them. After being trailed for some 2 miles (3.2 km) the brothers decided to stop their truck and see what happened. The object continued to advance until it was about 200 yds (180 m) from their vehicle, then it hovered briefly before coming down to land on the dust road.

Taking quick stock of the situation, the brothers decided to flee. They restarted their truck and made

In 1953, a remote road in the Australian outback was the scene for one of the first reports of a UFO landing.

off as fast as they could. This time the object did not follow them.

The incident raised a number of questions for researchers. The object had quite clearly been following the truck, but whether it had been attracted to the truck or the humans was unknown. Nor was it obvious why it had given up the pursuit when the brothers stopped. As to whether the motive for the chase had been hostile, curiosity or something else, was purely a matter for speculation.

Another early report of a saucer landing also came from Australia, this time from Claypans in South Australia. The postmaster, Mr C. Towill, was travelling with a carrier, Mr P. Briggs, out of Claypans towards Adelaide at around 2 am. It was Towill who first saw the object resting in a field about 400 yds (365 m) from the road. It was bigger than a passenger airliner and glowed with a strange inner light that seemed to diffuse out from its surface. Towill later compared the effect to the light of a torch glowing through the walls of a canvas tent. The object was studded with a number of small, round lights that pulsated between red and blue.

The two humans halted their vehicle and sat watching the object. After about ten minutes, they decided to investigate. They had got to within 200 yds (180 m) of the object when, in Towill's words, 'we both felt that something inside the craft was aware of our presence and was watching us'. The two men stopped advancing and watched warily. The object

rose slowly into the air, hovered silently for a few seconds, then accelerated rapidly and climbed away at great speed.

Again, speculation as to what had been going on was rife. The saucer, which was of the 'cigar-shape' configuration, had been stationary on the ground for at least 10 minutes, and had possibly been there for much longer before Towill and Briggs arrived on the

> ## 'The object ... was bigger than a passenger airliner and glowed with a strange inner light that seemed to diffuse out from its surface.'

scene. Perhaps the craft and its occupants had been studying something, maybe they were resting – or were they waiting for a human vehicle to come along the nearby road? Whatever they had been up to, the occupants had clearly not welcomed the interest of the two humans and had left when they got too close.

There was a series of incidents involving UFOs taking an apparent interest in civilian aircraft in the early 1950s. At the time UFO researchers placed a great deal of importance on these events. This was partly because they showed a clear interaction between the UFO and the aircraft that seemed to indicate that an intelligent being was controlling the UFO. Perhaps even more important for the researchers was the fact that aircrew are almost by definition experienced at seeing things in the sky and could be relied upon not to mistake a mundane object for something mysterious.

On 19 October 1953, for instance, an American Airlines DC6 flying out of Washington DC encountered a UFO over Maryland. The pilot, J.L. Kidd, first saw the object when it was some miles away. The UFO then changed direction and charged straight at the DC6. Kidd threw the aircraft into a sudden dive to avoid a collision. The manoeuvre was so sudden and violent that several passengers were thrown out of their

> **'Kidd threw the aircraft into a sudden dive to avoid a collision. The manoeuvre was so sudden and violent that several passengers were thrown out of their seats.'**

seats. Kidd diverted back to Washington so that medical staff could tend to the passengers, though it turned out that none had been badly injured.

Rather more serious were the results of a similar encounter over Long Beach, California, between a United Airlines flight and a UFO on 14 April 1954. Again the UFO made a deliberate turn so as to approach the aircraft on a collision course. The pilot J. M. Schidel threw his aircraft into a steep climbing turn. One passenger suffered a broken leg while the stewardess broke her ankle.

CLAMP-DOWN

Perhaps as a result of this incident, but certainly because of the general media coverage being given to reports by pilots, the US Joint Chiefs of Staff took it upon themselves to expand the scope and seriousness of regulations issued under the Espionage Laws then in force. These laws had long made it an offence for anyone to reveal to the public or an unauthorized person any fact that a senior military officer had instructed them to keep secret. The purpose of the regulations was simply to make it illegal for a civilian to pass on information that he had acquired accidentally or through his work. There was nothing sinister about them at all.

However, instructions were now issued to all civilian airlines, stating that the regulations now covered all reports of UFOs. Any member of an aircrew who revealed an encounter with a UFO to anyone other than a military official risked a fine of $10,000 or up to ten years in prison.

It was a heavy-handed response to the situation, but it did have the effect of reducing drastically the number of reports made by aircrew becoming public. It also added to the conviction that was now becoming widespread among UFO researchers that the US government in general, and the USAF in particular, knew far more about UFOs than they were letting on.

Of course, the new regulations affected only US airline companies. Aircrew working for other companies continued to make reports. On 29 June

More than one passenger airliner has been forced to take violent evasive action to avoid a collision with a UFO.

1954 the British Overseas Airways Corporation flight from New York to London was cruising over Quebec at about 19,000 ft (5,800 m) when the pilot, James Howard, saw something odd.

Although partial cloud rather obscured his view, Howard realized that his aircraft was being accompanied by a number of objects flying on a parallel course, some 8,000 ft (2,450 m) lower and about 3 miles (5.5 km) to port. When the aircraft crossed the Canadian coast the cloud cleared, and Howard and his crew were able to study their mysterious escorts more clearly. There was a large

craft, accompanied by six smaller objects. The six smaller craft kept close to the larger object, but constantly changed their relative positions.

After about ten minutes of this, Howard called up Goose Bay Airport on Labrador on his radio to ask for advice. The air traffic controller replied that the BOAC aircraft was out of radar range of Goose Bay, but that a USAF F94 fighter that was on a routine patrol in the area had been alerted and would rendezvous with Howard's aircraft. Howard then switched to the USAF radio frequency to talk directly to the fighter pilot to give him the current position of the airliner and the intruders.

Meanwhile the mysterious companions had been altering formation. Howard had been busy on the radio, but the navigator had been watching. The six small objects had circled around, then converged on the larger object and disappeared from view. He thought that they may have entered the large object somehow, but could not be certain.

As the F94 converged on Howard's aircraft the remaining UFO began to behave in what can only be called a bizarre fashion. Although remaining apparently solid and with a colour that indicated it was made of a greyish metal, the UFO began to alter shape. Then it shrank in size. In front of the bemused eyes of Howard, his crew and passengers, it simply faded out of sight. By the time the F94 came within range of its air-to-air combat radar there was nothing for it to lock on to.

Howard was later interviewed by investigators from the USAF. He was questioned closely and at some length, but he got the impression that the officers were not really interested. It was almost as if they had heard it all so many times before that they were merely recording the details for form's sake.

A number of reports have accumulated that indicate that UFOs or their crews take an interest in

'The UFO ... shrank in size. In front of the bemused eyes of Howard, his crew and passengers, it simply faded out of sight.'

human military bases, and the more secretive the bases are the more interested the UFOs appear to be. One of the classic cases of this kind occurred in December 1980 at Rendlesham forest in Suffolk.

RENDLESHAM

The large pine forest of Rendlesham is bordered to the east by the North Sea coast, on which stands the long peninsula of Orford Ness. In 1980 the peninsula was occupied by a top secret military base manned by American personnel. On the far end of the Ness stands a lighthouse. To the western end of the forest stood, in 1980, two USAF airfields: Bentwaters and Woodbridge, from which flew bombers and fighters active in patrolling the North Sea to watch out for Soviet intruders during the Cold War. The events that unfolded at Rendlesham that year were subjected to the usual USAF secrecy and had to be pieced together later.

The incident began some time towards midnight – the precise time is uncertain – with a sighting by Gordon Levett. Levett, who lived near the village of Sudbourne, took his dog out into the garden and was disturbed by a bright light from the otherwise dark, but clear sky. He looked up to see an unusual object passing silently overhead. He later described it as being 'shaped like a mushroom' and emitting an eerie greenish-white light. The object seemed to pause almost over his house before moving off in the direction of the Woodbridge air base.

The dense Rendlesham forest was the site of a classic British UFO encounter in 1980.

Some time after midnight (again the precise time is unclear) the Webb family were driving home from a party. They were passing down the lane that runs from Orford to Woodbridge when the road was bathed in a greenish-white light. Peering up into the sky, they saw a large object that was quite different from the usual military aircraft that they often saw flying about the area. The object was heading for Woodbridge, then it seemed to accelerate and dive towards the ground, passing out of sight behind the trees of Rendlesham forest.

David Roberts was parked up a secluded dirt track leading off the lane, with his girlfriend. They too saw the object fly overhead and then felt a distinct bump as whatever it was hit the ground somewhere near them amid the trees.

At around 1.50 am USAF guards Bud Parker and John Burroughs were on duty at the east gate of Woodbridge air base. They saw a glowing object approaching the base from over Rendlesham forest. They said that it was shaped like a Christmas tree. As they watched, the object suddenly dived down into the forest itself, which was then illuminated with a blaze of flashing lights. Burroughs called up the main guardhouse to report the incident. The call was logged at 2 am, the first firm time fix for the sighting.

Sergeant Jim Penniston and Herman Kavanasac were dispatched from the guardhouse to investigate.

An artist's impression of the UFO that landed in Rendlesham forest, based on eyewitness accounts of those in the forest that night.

After a few words with Burroughs and Parker, they raced into the woods in their jeep with headlights blazing and sirens wailing. The vehicle careered past Roberts and his girlfriend who, deciding something serious was afoot, left at once.

Once in the forest, Penniston studied the coloured, flashing lights for a few minutes and decided that an aircraft had crashed. He went back to the post guarded by Burroughs and Parker, who disagreed with him, saying that the object had seemed to land gently, not crash. Together the four men went back into Rendlesham forest to investigate further.

Penniston soon found that his radio was not working properly, the signals being swamped by static. He sent Kavanasac back to wait on the edge of the forest where the static was not so bad. Penniston gave Kavanasac orders to relay messages between Woodbridge and himself so long as he could.

It was Penniston and Burroughs who found the source of the disturbance as they pushed on into the forest. Coming into a clearing the two men found themselves confronted by an object about 30 ft (9 m) across that was shaped rather like a cone. It was resting on legs, according to Burroughs, while Penniston thought that it was hovering and shining bright lights down to the ground.

The two men glanced uneasily at each other for a few seconds. Then Penniston began to advance. He later likened the experience to walking through molasses. Although he was willing his body to move, there seemed to be some force holding him back. Every step was a struggle.

Penniston had barely advanced 10 ft (3 m) towards the object when it emitted a blindingly bright flash of light. Recovering their sight, the two men saw the craft rising upwards and accelerating rapidly. The flash seemed to have awoken every wild animal in the forest and the air was filled with the noise of birds squawking and calling, and of mammals crashing through the undergrowth. The object flew off at speed until it faded from sight.

Next day USAF personnel came out of Woodbridge to investigate the site of the encounter in more detail. They found that the tops of several trees had been smashed off as if something very heavy had flown so low as to clip them. In the clearing were three indentations that matched the positions of the legs or light beams coming from the object. Perhaps most interesting was the fact that the site gave off high levels of radiation.

One other thing was discovered that morning. Gordon Levett found his dog was ill. He took it to the

'... they massed a team of men armed with arc lights, geiger counters, infra-red night goggles and other search equipment.'

local vet, who thought that perhaps the dog had been poisoned, but could not identify any specific ailment. Three days later the dog died.

Because the events of the night had taken place outside the USAF base they were officially the responsibility of the British authorities. The USAF base commander alerted the British Ministry of Defence and the local police. Suffolk police turned up

promptly, roped off the clearing and began taking measurements and plaster casts of the indentations. Then the investigation was abruptly called off. The men on the ground later said that the orders to cease work at Rendlesham had come from very high up the chain of command.

That evening, 26 December, flashing lights again came out of Rendlesham forest. This time they were seen by the guards at Bentwaters air base. Base commander Ted Conrad called head of security, Lieutenant Bruce Englund, and together they massed a team of men armed with arc lights, geiger counters, infra-red night goggles and other search equipment. Hearing what was afoot, John Burroughs raced over from Woodbridge to join the search.

By the time the search party set off into the forest, led by Conrad's deputy Lieutenant Colonel Charles Halt, the lights had stopped flashing. However the watching guards had seen nothing leave and were convinced that whatever 'it' was, it was still somewhere in the forest. This supposition was reinforced by the fact that the search team's radios began to crackle with static and rapidly became inoperative as the men pushed into the forest.

At first little could be seen in the dark, night-time woodland. Halt had a Dictaphone on him and kept up a running commentary. He ordered his men to spread out and move forward slowly toward the spot where the guards had estimated the lights to be coming from. They were some 200 ft (60 m) into the woods when the Geiger counter began rising rapidly. It levelled off at around ten times the normal background readings. This was high, but not dangerous. Halt ordered his men on.

The infra-red goggles picked up a heat source somewhere ahead. At around 1.50 am a light was seen through the trees. Halt told his men to advance warily. Sergeant Adrian Bustinza was closest to the mystery light, which he described as looking like a dull light bulb perched on top of a mist, emitting a dull yellowish glow. Then red flashing lights began to spark out from the object. Halt thought the lights were on the move, coming toward him. He commented on his Dictaphone, 'This is weird'. As the light approached it could be seen to have a dark centre.

Then the object began to move away through the trees. Halt ordered his men to advance once again. They followed the object out of the wood, over a field and through a stream. Suddenly, at 3.15 am, the object began to rise quickly up into the sky. It shone a bright beam down to the ground. That was broken off and was followed by a series of what seemed to be laser beams lancing out through the darkness. Some of the beams came close to Halt and his men, one striking the ground only inches from where Halt was standing. Thinking they were under attack, Halt ordered his men to take cover. But the object, whatever it was, seemed to lose interest and flew off.

Meanwhile, the radar station at nearby RAF Watton had been tracking the flying object. The object did not give off any of the recognized radar response signals and could not be raised on radio. As the radar operators pondered the mystery signal, it suddenly accelerated to unbelievable speeds and raced out of range.

'... so many people had seen the lights and been involved in the search parties that news did slowly leak out that something odd had happened ...'

Three days later senior USAF officers arrived at RAF Watton armed with authority from the British Ministry of Defence to impound all radar records for the Christmas period. A similar team from the USAF took the radar records from RAF Neatishead. The records were never returned. A secret flight came into Woodbridge about this time carrying a team of USAF intelligence officers. Their mission has never been explained. A news blackout on the events was imposed at the request of the USAF.

Nevertheless, so many people had seen the lights and been involved in the search parties that news did slowly leak out that something odd had happened in Rendlesham forest over Christmas. Others, not directly involved, noticed odd things. A forestry worker, for instance, found that numerous trees around a clearing – later identified as being the one where the object had rested on the first night – had been felled and taken away even though they were some years away from being fit for harvesting.

By the spring of 1981, UFO researchers had come to believe that a UFO had landed in Rendlesham forest and had been approached by US military personnel. Beyond that details were vague. Neither the USAF nor the British Ministry of Defence was willing to confirm or deny events. It was not until three years later that the first official documents relating to the event were extracted from unwilling authorities using Freedom of Information legislation, and more years dragged by before the details came out.

Even now, rumours persist that the more dramatic evidence remains suppressed. Some believe that humanoids linked to the UFO were seen in the forest. Others that the UFO left behind physical evidence of its passing.

However, the authorities have sought to explain events by linking them to a bright shooting star, or meteor, that flew across southern England at 2.50 am on the night of 26 December. It is suggested that this dramatic event triggered the alarm, and that the search parties subsequently mistook the flashing light from the Orford Ness lighthouse for a downed UFO in the forest.

In response it must be pointed out that the mystery object was seen well before 2.50 am, and in any case no meteor was reported for the previous night. Nor is it credible that men who had lived on the air base for some months were likely to mistake a distant lighthouse that they saw every night for something unexplained.

The events at Rendlesham forest remain a mystery. The fact that the USAF and Britain's Ministry of Defence tried to cover up the very occurrence of an event would seem to indicate that they very much wanted the truth to remain hidden. Perhaps they have succeeded.

MYSTERY VISITORS

Other reports of saucers landing or the visitors apparently taking an interest in humans continued to accumulate. Generally the events did not allow for any firm conclusions to be drawn. Some researchers felt that the mysterious occupants were merely curious about humans. Others thought that the beings were rather more indifferent. A few thought that the intruders were hostile. At this date, nearly all agreed that the beings that controlled the UFOs were engaged on some sort of reconnaissance mission.

It was generally expected that in the near future the saucer operators would choose to reveal their purpose to humanity. Until then reports continued to be collected and analyzed. And everyone speculated about what the inhabitants of the saucers looked like.

In fact, some people claimed to have already seen the beings that operated the UFOs. The problem for researchers was that many of these witnesses were reluctant to talk publicly about their experiences, and many did not want to talk about them at all. This meant that some reports never became known outside of a tight family circle, while others could be published only

DEPARTMENT OF THE AIR FORCE
HEADQUARTERS 81ST COMBAT SUPPORT GROUP (USAFE)
APO NEW YORK 09755

REPLY TO
ATTN OF.   CD

13 Jan 81

SUBJECT: Unexplained Lights

TO: RAF/CC

1. Early in the morning of 27 Dec 80 (approximately 0300L), two USAF security police patrolmen saw unusual lights outside the back gate at RAF Woodbridge. Thinking an aircraft might have crashed or been forced down, they called for permission to go outside the gate to investigate. The on-duty flight chief responded and allowed three patrolmen to proceed on foot. The individuals reported seeing a strange glowing object in the forest. The object was described as being metalic in appearance and triangular in shape, approximately two to three meters across the base and approximately two meters high. It illuminated the entire forest with a white light. The object itself had a pulsing red light on top and a bank(s) of blue lights underneath. The object was hovering or on legs. As the patrolmen approached the object, it maneuvered through the trees and disappeared. At this time the animals on a nearby farm went into a frenzy. The object was briefly sighted approximately an hour later near the back gate.

2. The next day, three depressions 1 1/2" deep and 7" in diameter were found where the object had been sighted on the ground. The following night (29 Dec 80) the area was checked for radiation. Beta/gamma readings of 0.1 milliroentgens were recorded with peak readings in the three depressions and near the center of the triangle formed by the depressions. A nearby tree had moderate (.05-.07) readings on the side of the tree toward the depressions.

3. Later in the night a red sun-like light was seen through the trees. It moved about and pulsed. At one point it appeared to throw off glowing particles and then broke into five separate white objects and then disappeared. Immediately thereafter, three star-like objects were noticed in the sky, two objects to the north and one to the south, all of which were about 10° off the horizon. The objects moved rapidly in sharp angular movements and displayed red, green and blue lights. The objects to the north appeared to be elliptical through an 8-12 power lens. They then turned to full circles. The objects to the north remained in the sky for an hour or more. The object to the south was visible for two or three hours and beamed down a stream of light from time to time. Numerous individuals, including the undersigned, witnessed the activities in paragraphs 2 and 3.

CHARLES I. HALT, Lt Col, USAF
Deputy Base Commander

The initial report by Lt Col Charles Halt on the Rendlesham incident. Other details would emerge later.

with the name of the witness kept secret. Inevitably the presence of a sole witness who remained anonymous undermined the credibility of the report.

Even those few early reports of beings emerging from saucers that did get published were often discounted. The witness was very often not very well educated and, no matter how sincere or otherwise credible, this fact was often used by sceptics to dismiss the report.

A few examples will serve to illustrate the difficulties encountered by researchers investigating early reports during the 1950s.

One of the earliest came out of Steep Rock, Ontario, in September 1950. The two witnesses, who preferred to remain anonymous, were a mining manager and his wife who were on vacation on the shores of Lake Ontario. On 2 July they had been out boating and pulled into a small cove to eat a packed lunch and relax. Suddenly the couple felt the earth rock and the air shake, as if there were an explosion nearby – though no blast was heard.

The couple climbed a short rise to see what lay beyond, as the air blast had seemed to come from that direction. About 400 yds (365 m) away they saw a round, silver, shiny object apparently floating on the water by the shoreline. It seemed to be about 50 ft (15 m) across with portholes around the edge and an open hatchway on its upper surface.

Walking about on the upper surface of the saucer were ten figures. Each figure was roughly human in

In 1950 a holidaying couple saw humanoids emerging from a UFO on the shores of Lake Ontario.

shape, but they moved with odd movements. In particular they seemed unable to turn their heads, but had to shuffle laboriously round so that their whole bodies faced in the direction they wanted to look. The figures were about 4 ft (1.2 m) tall and dressed in a tight, one-piece outfit that was silvery in colour over the body but darker on the limbs. Their heads were encased in helmets of a reddish colour.

Projecting up from the centre of the saucer was a tall rod on which was mounted a continually rotating hoop-shaped device. At one point the hoop stopped suddenly, and all the figures stopped what they were doing to look in the direction it pointed. A few seconds later a deer emerged from a bush. The device resumed its rotating and the figures carried on working.

The witnesses could not see very clearly what the strange figures were doing, except that it involved carrying tubes and boxes about. One tube was slung over the side of the craft into the lake water, and the witnesses assumed that their craft was either taking on water or pumping out waste material of some kind.

After some minutes the figures retreated back into the saucer, taking their equipment with them. The saucer took off, leaving a reddish-blue stain on the water where it had rested, and flew off at speed.

Rather more disturbing was the encounter that took place on 23 February 1955 when a bricklayer named Fred Biggs was cycling to his work on a building site near the town of Romsey in Hampshire. As he passed a field beside a stream he noticed an object hovering silently over the grass. Biggs stopped, dismounted and began to approach the object.

He could see that it was circular, about 30 ft (9 m) in diameter and coloured a sort of dull silver or brushed aluminium. Around its rim was a row of what looked like windows or portholes. It was about 100 yds (90 m) away from Biggs and some 60 ft (18 m) off the ground.

As Biggs watched, a tube or rod emerged from the underside of the saucer. Attached to it was a small platform, on which stood a figure. The figure was basically humanoid, but rather small. It was dressed in what seemed to be a dark, one-piece suit and had

The crew of the UFO seen at Lake Ontario put a pipe into the lake as if sucking up water.

a hat or helmet on its head. It was then that one of the porthole-like openings emitted a bright blue flash. Biggs felt as if he had been hit very hard by some large, heavy object. He fell over backwards to lie in the snow that covered the field. Although he remained fully conscious, Biggs was unable to move either his arms or his legs.

Craning his head round to look at the saucer, Biggs saw the figure, platform and tube retracted back into the underside of the craft. The saucer then rose vertically, rapidly gaining speed until it shot into the cloud cover with the speed of a jet aircraft. It emitted a soft, whooshing sound as it did so.

After a few seconds, Biggs was suddenly able to move. He got back on his bike and cycled to work where he found his mate Ron Heath waiting for him. Biggs hurriedly told Heath what had happened, and together the two men hurried back to the field to look for evidence. The footprints left by Biggs could be made out, as could the marks in the snow where he had lain. There were no marks left by the UFO, but then Biggs had not seen it actually land. There did seem to be rather more melting of the snow in the area where the UFO had hovered, but that was about it.

The two men were, as a result, late getting to work. When they told their employer what had happened, he asked them to write down the details of the event, which they did.

> ### 'It was then that one of the porthole-like openings emitted a bright blue flash. Biggs felt as if he had been hit very hard by some large, heavy object.'

With signed statements written within hours of an encounter with the occupant of a flying saucer, it might be thought that the case would be seized upon by researchers as evidence that living beings were piloting the UFOs. However, neither of the men involved was willing to have their names released at the time and only an edited version of their statements was made public. The full story did not emerge until 1979, by which time it had rather been overtaken by events.

FRENCH ENCOUNTER

Rather the opposite problem hampered a sighting of humanoids and a UFO that emerged from France in 1954. On the evening of 10 September, some three hours after dark, a farmer named Marius Dewilde who lived near Quarouble, close to the Belgian border, heard his dogs barking and howling. Picking up a torch, Dewilde stepped outside into his farmyard to see what the problem was.

Standing barely 12 ft (4 m) away from him was a human-like figure something under 4 ft (1.2 m) in height. A short distance further away was a second figure. At the time, events moved very quickly, but speaking later Dewilde described the figures as having legs rather too short for their height, with broad shoulders and abnormally large heads. He said that they had been dressed in tight, one-piece suits of the sort worn by divers of the time. Dewilde did not see any arms, but as he himself accepted he had only a second or so to take in the surprising and alarming sight before things began to happen.

The nearer of the two figures turned sharply to face Dewilde. The beam of the Frenchman's torch struck the being full in the face, but glanced off as if it had struck a mirror. Dewilde thought maybe that this was the visor of a helmet of some kind, which might have explained the large size of the heads.

Dewilde then caught sight of a large, dark object resting on the nearby railway lines. He glanced towards the object, and was instantly struck by a beam of intense light that erupted from it. Dewilde was both blinded by the light and instantly paralyzed. When the light went out the two figures had gone. The large object rose slowly into the air with a low-pitched whooshing sound.

For a few minutes, Dewilde remained unable to move. Then suddenly he recovered control of his limbs. He ran over a mile to the village to hammer on the doors of the local policeman. Dewilde was almost beside himself with fear and excitement. At first the policeman thought Dewilde had gone mad, then that he was drunk. Only after the farmer had calmed down

> **'Later investigations found deep indentations in the ground beside the railway lines on the spot where Dewilde said the object had rested.'**

a bit did the policeman take his story at all seriously.

Later investigations found deep indentations in the ground beside the railway lines on the spot where Dewilde said the object had rested. The depth of the marks indicated that the object had weighed something over 25 tons.

With physical marks left behind by the landed UFO and a witness willing to talk on the record, this case had the potential to offer real evidence. Unfortunately, Dewilde was something less than a reliable witness. As a poorly educated rural peasant farmer, he was an easy target for the sceptics. Added to that was the fact that the dramatic events had a profound effect on him. He simply could not stop talking about them, often at great speed and in a state of excitement. Within weeks, however, Dewilde had changed. He became truculent and refused to talk to anyone about the incident. He made a poor witness.

ARMED CLASH

Also reluctant to talk about their experiences were the Sutton family of Hopkinsville, Kentucky, who had their utterly bizarre and truly terrifying encounter on 21 August 1955. Their desire for privacy was hardly surprising, for once word got out about what had happened the Sutton farm was besieged by sightseers, reporters and other assorted nuisances.

The events began when a UFO was seen to land near the farm by one of the Suttons in the late afternoon. By dusk the entire extended family of eleven were gathered in the farmhouse for supper when the dogs began barking and howling. Two of the men went to the door to see what was causing the fuss. They saw a strange figure walking toward the house across the field.

The intruder was just over 3 ft (1 m) tall and emitted a pale glow that seemed to come from all over its body. It did not seem to be wearing clothes of any kind. The creature had huge ears, that ended in sharp points at top and bottom. The head was large and highly domed, but had a small chin, a tiny nose and a mere slit as a mouth. The body was thin and tapered sharply from the wide shoulders to the thin waist that sat on short, spindly legs. The arms were over-long, ended in talon-like claws and were being held threateningly overhead.

Understandably startled, the two men watched the creature approaching in silence. Then the elder man decided to take some positive action. He stepped back into the house, picked up his shotgun and returned to the doorway as the approaching creature was just 20 ft (6 m) away. Lifting the gun to his shoulder he blasted the creature. The being flipped over backwards and lay still on the ground. Then, incredibly, it simply got up and walked away, apparently uninjured.

Now other similar creatures appeared. When one climbed on to the roof of the farmhouse it was shot down with a rifle, but again was unhurt. The terrified Suttons barricaded themselves into their house, shooting at any of the strange creatures whenever they saw them. After some two hours of gunplay, the Suttons decided to flee. They piled into a car and raced for the safety of a nearby town. The beings did not pursue them. When the family returned to the farm a few hours later with armed police in tow, the intruders had gone.

At first the Suttons were happy to co-operate with both police and UFO researchers who called. All eleven family members were consistent both about what had happened and about the appearance and behaviour of

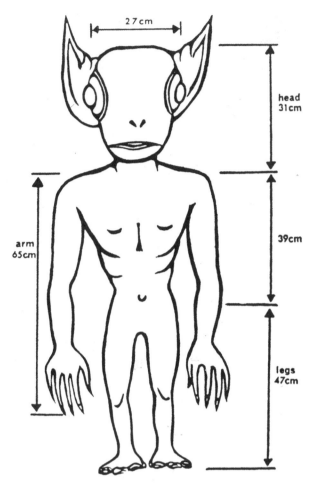

The original sketch of one of the aliens that attacked the Sutton family in Kentucky in 1955, drawn the day after the attack.

the humanoids. They even drew pictures of the things that had attacked them. The case had the potential to provide good evidence about the crew of the UFOs. But then news of the events was broadcast on the local radio station and following that, picked up by the national media. Soon the farm was inundated with visitors, both friendly and hostile. The Suttons closed ranks and refused to talk any further.

It was an absence of media, not an excess of it, that rendered an otherwise classic case from Italy

The Suttons, a family of Kentucky farmers, blasted at the aliens that attacked their home with rifles and shotguns.

virtually useless. On 24 April 1950 Bruno Facchini was sitting up fairly late in the evening at his remote country home near Varese. He caught sight of sparking lights outside that he thought must be lightning, though he then discounted this as there was no storm going on. Opening the door to see what was happening, Facchini came to a sudden halt when he saw the source of the lights.

About a 100 ft (30 m) away beside a telegraph pole there was a round object about 30 ft (9 m) across that

seemed to be made of metal. In the side of the object was an opening through which Facchini could see what looked like dials, controls and cylinders. He did not pay too much attention to the interior of the craft, for standing around it were four humanoids.

Each of the figures was about 5 ft (1.5 m) or more in height and was dressed in a tight-fitting grey overall. The heads of the figures were enclosed in helmets which featured transparent face masks. From each mask emerged a tube that ran down to a

'The object emitted a beam of bluish light that struck Facchini in the chest. The hapless Italian was hurled backward ...'

pack on the chest. Facchini took the tubes to be linked to breathing in some way.

The figures were all equipped with what looked like tools and seemed to be tinkering with the craft, though Facchini could not make out exactly what they were doing. He thought that they might be undertaking repairs and decided to offer to help.

As Facchini stepped forward from his front door, the beings seemed to notice him for the first time. They turned toward him, then began chattering to each other in a harsh-sounding language that Facchini had never heard before. One of the figures then pointed a

tube-like object at him. The object emitted a beam of bluish light that struck Facchini in the chest. The hapless Italian was hurled backward as if by some powerful force and sent sprawling on the ground.

Dazed, Facchini sat up just in time to see the last of the beings stepping through the opening and back into the craft. The door then closed, the object began to hum and it rose steadily into the air before flying off at high speed.

Facchini retreated to his house, bolted the doors and settled down to wait for dawn. When daylight came he emerged to find that the previous night's intruders had gone. They had left behind scorch marks on the ground and indentations where the saucer had apparently rested on legs.

Facchini was a credible witness of extraordinary events. Unfortunately the incident was reported only

Several UFOs, such as that seen by Bruno Facchini in 1950, have been spotted near or over electricity power cables.

in local newspapers and did not come to the attention of researchers until many years later.

A similar problem of remoteness bedevilled the sighting of humanoids by Father William Gill, a missionary working at a remote station on Mount Pudi, Papua New Guinea. His encounter took place on 26 June 1959, but it was to be ten years before it became widely known.

At about 7 pm a large flying object shaped rather like two plates placed rim to rim came drifting down through the cloud cover that Gill estimated to be at around 2,000 ft (600 m). Neither Gill nor any of his

Father Gill and his New Guinea workers waved to the crew of a UFO that appeared over their mission in 1959.

local converts knew very much about aircraft and did not realize that they were seeing anything very unusual. They assumed that the craft was some sort of modern flying machine, perhaps operated by the USAF which had bases on the island.

> ## 'Thinking that his visitors were going to land ... Gill waved hello. One of the figures on the UFO looked down at him and waved back.'

The object had what looked like a deck running around the outer edge of its upper side. A pair of human-like figures emerged from the craft and began walking about on the decking. They then began working with what seemed to be tools or devices of some kind. Thinking that his visitors were going to land on the large flat field over which the object was hovering, Gill waved hello. One of the figures on the UFO looked down at him and waved back.

The object made no move to land, so Gill and the villagers with him assumed that the crew was neither in trouble nor intended to pay a visit. Gill went off to eat his dinner. The crew of the flying object and the villagers continued to exchange waves for some time. Then the craft rose up into the cloud cover and disappeared from view.

Numerous other incidents occurred during the 1950s that emerged only through anonymous witnesses. Although they were of great interest to UFO researchers, the fact that the witnesses refused to be named – as in the following cases – detracted from the value of their accounts.

On 5 October 1954 a teenage boy living on a farm near Loctudy in France was sent out by his family to draw water from the well, which stood a few yards from the house. The boy was amazed when a luminous, disc-shaped object flew down to land silently barely 20 ft (6 m) away. A door opened and out stepped a humanoid figure about 3 ft (1 m) high that had a face covered in hair.

The strange figure approached the boy, touched him on the arm and began speaking in a strange language. It seemed surprised that the boy could not understand him, and seemed to be asking a question of some kind. Giving up in apparent disgust, the figure reboarded the UFO and flew off.

RABBIT ABDUCTION

On 14 November of the same year, an Italian farmer near Isola saw an oval object land near his farm. Three short humanoids, about 4 ft (1.2 m) tall emerged. They were wearing what looked like jumpsuits made of a soft metallic fabric. The figures pottered about, unconcerned by the watching farmer. One of the figures then spotted a hutch of rabbits that the farmer was breeding and called over its companions. The trio then went over to the hutch, pointing excitedly at the rabbits and conversing in a language the farmer could not understand.

When one of the beings made to open the cage and take out a rabbit, the farmer decided that things had gone far enough. He darted back into his house, picked up a rifle and came back out. Pointing the rifle at the intruders he ordered them to leave his rabbits alone. One of the beings glanced at the farmer, whereupon the gun became so heavy that the farmer had to drop it. Cradling a rabbit in its arms one of the intruders walked off back to its craft, while the other two kept an eye on the farmer. Climbing back into the craft, the visitors then flew off.

One case that did benefit from some official investigation – albeit rather cursory – came in 1962 when the Argentine police released a report into a

Rabbits were the surprising victims of the aliens that visited an Italian farm in 1954.

> **'The figures moved slowly away from the craft, looking down at the ground and apparently inspecting the foliage of the plants.'**

UFO sighting. On 24 May a disc-shaped UFO had landed near a range outside the town of La Pampa. A door had opened in the side of the craft and out stepped a pair of humanoid figures that moved with a jerky, awkward motion. The ranch hands who witnessed the event thought that the visitors were robots. The figures moved slowly away from the craft, looking down at the ground and apparently inspecting the foliage of the plants. Then one of them happened to glance at the ranch house and saw the men watching. At once the two robot figures walked jerkily back to their craft, got in and flew off.

When the police arrived a few hours later they took statements from the witnesses, all of which tallied closely, and went to inspect the landing site. They found a circular area about 18 ft (5.5 m) across where all the grass had been scorched to ashes. Nearby bushes had their leaves singed.

ABORIGINAL MYSTERY

In 1951 an incident occurred that did not reach the world's press until some seven months after the event. Although it is not talked about much today, at the time it made a real impact as it was the first time that people from a non-Western culture reported what was undoubtedly a UFO landing, complete with what seemed to be a crew member. Some time in September – the precise date was never made clear – a band of the Unmatjera tribe of Australian Aborigines was moving through the Stansmore Ranges of central Australia. The tribe was, at this date, not yet settled on a reserve. They largely followed their traditional lifestyles, though they stopped off at government stations to take advantage of healthcare from time to time, while the men would go to work on ranches for a while to earn money to buy various goods.

> **'In the shallow valley beneath them they saw a large metal vehicle that they took to be something to do with European civilization.'**

On this particular day, four of the tribe's men were out hunting when they came to the top of a low ridge. In the shallow valley beneath them they saw a large metal vehicle that they took to be something to do with European civilization. Seeing no sign of any movement, the men sat down to watch from cover. The object was around 50 ft (15 m) across, 10 ft (3 m) tall in the centre and rounded in shape.

After some minutes a second, almost identical object came drifting down from above with a buzzing sound, akin to a swarm of bees but much louder. It came to rest close to the first object. A door opened in the side of the new arrival and a figure emerged. The figure was about 4 ft (1.2 m) tall, wore a shiny red outfit and had a large, round, shiny head – perhaps he was wearing a helmet of some kind. The figure walked to the first saucer and climbed in through a hatch. The hatches on both saucers then slammed shut and the two saucers flew off.

The Unmatjera band reported the incident the next time they stopped at a government station, thinking that the event they had witnessed might be of interest. Then they walked off again into the outback. By the time reporters heard the story, the witnesses had gone and could not be questioned. Nevertheless, the story was afforded a lot of publicity as it showed that it was not only Westerners watching science fiction movies who saw flying saucers.

A VIOLENT MEETING

Not all witnesses were content merely to watch what was happening. Jose Ponce and Gustavo Gonzales decided to be considerably more pro-active, almost aggressive, when they encountered a UFO and its occupant near Petare, Venezuela, on 28 November 1954. The two men were driving a truck down a rural road late at night when they found their route blocked by a glowing, saucer-shaped object hovering just above the road surface.

The men stopped their truck and got out to get a better look. When they got to about 25 ft (7.5 m) away, they saw that a humanoid some 4 ft (1.2 m) tall and covered in hair had emerged and was walking toward

The Aborigine hunters who saw two huge UFOs land in the Australian outback in 1951 took them to be European aircraft.

them. Gonzales reacted first, lunging at the figure and lifting it clear of the ground – he later said that he thought it weighed around 3 stone (20 kg).

The humanoid clearly did not want to be treated like this. It squirmed out of Gonzales's grip, then turned and struck him so hard that he was sent sprawling backwards on the road. Ponce then fled for a police station he knew to be about a 1/4 mile (0.5 km) away.

Gonzales, meanwhile, was sitting upright on the road when the small figure hurled itself at him.

'Gonzales managed to pull his knife and slammed the blade into the creature's shoulder.'

shoulder. The blade glanced off as if it had hit metal sheet, but the blow did cause the creature to pull back.

A second creature now appeared, having presumably emerged from the UFO, and hurried forwards. It lifted a tube-like tool in its hand and pointed it at Gonzales. There was a sudden, blinding flash of light and Gonzales was helpless. Thinking he was done for, the young man lashed around with his knife but without hitting anything. When he could see again a couple of minutes later, Gonzales saw the UFO was now hovering some 30 ft (9 m) in the air. It then silently flew off out of sight.

Gonzales took to his heels and followed his friend to the police station. There Ponce had at first been treated with some scepticism, but when Gonzales arrived with blood pouring from his wounds the police changed their attitude. Gonzales was given medical treatment, a nasty cut down one side of his body giving some cause for concern. The doctors thought it had been caused by an animal's claw or a sharp hook of some kind – they did not accept the UFO story.

Interestingly, the story told by the two young men was later corroborated by a well-known local doctor who preferred to remain anonymous. He had been hurrying to a call when he drove past Gonzales standing in the road watching the departing UFO. The

Gonzales had time to notice that the figure's eyes gleamed yellow in the headlights of the truck, like those of a cat, before it was on him. Scratching and biting, the humanoid seemed intent on wrestling Gonzales on to his back. Gonzales managed to pull his knife and slammed the blade into the creature's

In 1954 Gustavo Gonzales was momentarily blinded during a fight with a pair of aliens. His knife had no effect on his opponents.

doctor had also seen the UFO, but was too intent on his call to stop. Not until the tale appeared in the local press did he come forward to talk to police.

SOCORRO: A CLASSIC CASE

Given this background of events and incidents it was with understandable relief that UFO researchers pounced on the Socorro Incident of 1964. The case involved witnesses of undoubted honesty, good observational skills and total reliability. With a UFO seen by two policemen and a relatively close up view of beings that emerged from the craft, news of the incident spread rapidly and it became a classic.

The main witness was Lonnie Zamora, a policeman based in Socorro, New Mexico. At 5.45 pm on 24 April 1964, Zamora was chasing a speeding motorist south of town when he heard an explosion and saw a sheet of blue flame soaring into the sky from behind a nearby hill. Knowing that a mining company kept dynamite in a store in that direction, Zamora feared that there had been an accident and went to investigate while calling for back-up.

Zamora's route took him along a dirt road over broken ground. As he approached the dynamite store Zamora was relieved to see it intact. He then saw a white object shaped like an elongated oval standing on one end. As he got closer he saw it had a red insignia like a truncated arrow painted on one side and was resting on short, stumpy legs. Beside the object were two short humanoid figures dressed in white.

Zamora then lost sight of the object behind a rise in the ground. As he drove up on to the rise he could again see the object, but the figures had gone. He was now only 50 yds (46 m) from the object, but the road now turned and went in the wrong direction.

Zamora halted his car and got out to approach on foot. As he did so he heard a series of loud bangs coming from the craft as if doors were being slammed shut. Blue flames began to emerge from the base of the craft, causing Zamora to dive for cover. Glancing up from behind a rock, Zamora watched the craft rise slowly into the sky and begin to move off. It was at this point that Sergeant Chavez, Zamora's back-up, arrived. He watched the craft speed off out of sight, but had got there too late to see the humanoids.

The Socorro Incident hit the headlines as the chief witness was a policeman of unimpeachable character.

The case caused a sensation. It demonstrated to many UFO researchers, and to others, that the UFOs were real mechanical craft that contained a crew. Zamora's fleeting glimpse indicated what these crew members looked like and how they behaved.

The figures were basically human in form, though they were very small at something between 3 and 4 ft (1–1.2 m) in height. They were dressed in fairly tight-fitting clothes that resembled overalls. Zamora thought that they had been wearing helmets of some kind, but could not provide details. Perhaps the intruders needed helmets to protect them against Earth's atmosphere.

If the purpose of the visit was unknown, the behaviour of the figures had been clear enough. When first seen they had been close to the landed UFO, but not apparently working on it or touching it in any way. If anything they had been looking around at their surroundings. Once Zamora had come into sight, however, the behaviour had changed markedly. The figures had climbed back into their UFO and made off at speed. Whatever they had been doing, they did not want to make direct contact with Zamora – nor presumably with any other human.

The most important effect of the Socorro case was to make it suddenly respectable to report seeing humanoid creatures in conjunction with UFOs. In the months and years that followed a host of reports were made of encounters with such creatures. Some of these reports were of new events and were made within days or even hours of their taking place. Others related to events in the past, but emerged now as the witnesses no longer feared ridicule so badly as they had done before. The press also picked up on previous incidents that had been reported by witnesses at the time but had been largely ignored.

One such incident involved French builder Georges Gatay. On 30 September 1954 he had been working on a site near Marcilly-sur-Vienne when a dome-shaped object that gave off a bright light came down to hover just above the ground a short distance away.

UFO investigators inspect the site of the Socorro landing where marks in the sand showed where the UFO had rested.

All the men on the site saw it and stopped work to stare. Only Gatay felt a strange compulsion to walk towards the object. A short humanoid figure appeared, as if he had stepped out from behind the craft. A beam of light came from a belt around his waist. Gatay had got quite close to the figure when it returned to the craft, which took off and flew rapidly out of sight.

Next day most of the men reported in sick, complaining of nausea and giddiness. The mystery illness did not last long and within 48 hours they were all back at work. Gatay, however, suffered difficulty sleeping for some weeks after his encounter.

'The Gatay Incident was the first hint that the beings that emerge from UFOs are able to control human beings in some way.'

The Gatay Incident was the first hint that the beings that emerge from UFOs are able to control human beings in some way. Gatay insisted that he had not wanted to walk toward the UFO, being as surprised and scared as were his workmates, but that he had felt an irresistible urge to do so.

Another incident occurred in October 1958 when a Senor Angelu was riding his motorcycle near Figueras, Spain. Angelu was watching the road and so failed to see much detail of the object that flew low overhead and plunged into nearby woodland. Fearing

that a light aircraft had crashed, Angelu leapt from his motorbike and pushed into the trees. He got close enough to see that the object was unlike any aircraft he had ever seen, nor had it crashed.

The rounded, disc-shaped object was resting lightly on the ground and two short figures were nearby. They were much shorter than adult humans and had outsized heads. They seemed to be fascinated by the local plant life, tearing off leaves and taking samples of twigs. Dropping under the cover of the undergrowth, Angelu watched the humanoids for about ten minutes. Then they returned to the craft, which took off and flew out of sight.

STANDING TALL

Although the beings seen in conjunction with UFOs were overwhelmingly conforming to a certain physical type, not all fitted into the pattern. Very different, for example, were the humanoids reported emerging from a UFO near the town of Belo Horizonte in Brazil on 28 August 1963.

The creatures were around 7 ft (2 m) tall and while they were basically humanoid, they had red skin, no hair, no nose, no mouth and only one eye. The UFO took the form of a transparent globe that emitted a dull, throbbing light. One of the figures floated out of the side of the globe and came drifting down to the ground, riding on a beam of light. One of the witnesses tried to throw a stone at the intruder, but his arm was paralyzed when struck by a shaft of light that emerged from the chest of the being. The visitor then returned to the UFO, which flew off at speed.

The Belo Horizonte sighting was considered to be bizarre at the time, and remains so today. It does not fit the general run of reports and descriptions. The fact that the three witnesses were all under the age of 14 and were all terrified by what had occurred might account for some discrepancies, but not for all of them.

Despite such odd cases, the overall picture that was emerging of the UFOnauts, or those beings that emerged from UFOs, was by the later 1960s becoming clear. The beings were generally human-like in shape. They walked upright on two legs, had two arms, a torso-body and a head. The head was usually larger than would be expected of a human, but it had a face with two eyes, a nose and mouth and, usually, two ears. They were short, generally around 3 or 4 ft (1–1.2 m) tall. Details in reports could vary a good deal. The figures might be hairy or bald, wear jumpsuit affairs or run around naked, and they might be grey, green or brown in colour. However, such discrepancies could be explained away by the fact that the witnesses were, understandably, startled by the sight of the intruders and often very scared.

Similarly the behaviour of most of the beings that emerged from UFOs was fitting into a pattern, though there were exceptions. The visitors were most often seen when they seemed to be unaware that humans were present. When they realized humans were on the scene, they left with every sign of hurry.

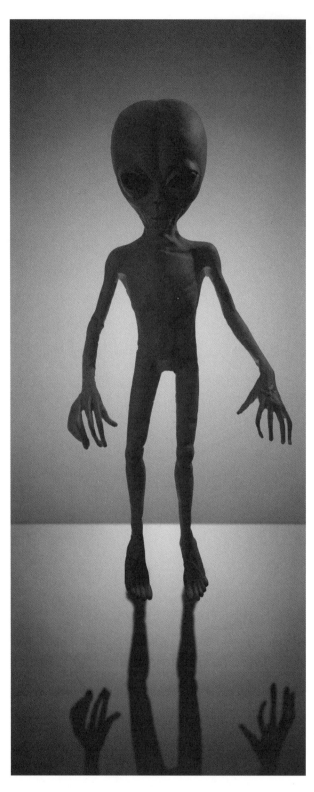

The image of the 'typical' alien as it emerged from sightings made in the 1960s and 1970s.

While undisturbed, the intruders seemed to behave as if deeply curious about the places where they had landed. They would poke about in fields and woods, peer into barns and inspect machinery with interest. They seemed to have a particular interest in plants and animals, whether wild or domesticated. Samples were sometimes taken and carried back to the UFO.

Some researchers thought that this behaviour was typical of explorers arriving on a strange planet for the first time. Comparisons were drawn with the way in which European sailors had behaved when arriving on Pacific islands for the first time in the 18th century.

Occasionally the UFOnauts might react aggressively to a human. They often paralyzed the human witness, knocked him over with some sort of a forcefield or rendered him unconscious. However, the witness did not seem to suffer any real long-term injuries, so such encounters could be interpreted as defensive actions rather than as outright attacks.

The only fatalities that could be ascribed to the mysterious beings were cases, such as that of Thomas Mantell, where the human was in a vehicle that crashed as a result of UFO activity. It is not certain that the UFOnauts would have known that crashing an aircraft would kill the pilot – they might not even have been aware the aircraft was manned as they may have taken it to be a missile of some kind.

Most researchers in the 1950s and 1960s were

'... the witness did not seem to suffer any real long-term injuries, so such encounters could be interpreted as defensive actions rather than as outright attacks.'

willing to give the UFOnauts the benefit of the doubt. It was assumed that whoever they were and whatever they wanted, they were not hostile to humanity. Some thought that they might be indifferent to the point of callousness – swatting a human aside with no more thought than a human might flatten a fly – but even so, not deliberately violent.

That was, however, about as far as any researchers were willing to go. While most thought that the UFOnauts were aliens from another planet, and that the UFOs were spacecraft, the origin of the craft and their purpose for coming to Earth were generally thought to be unknown. Perhaps, it was thought, time would tell. Maybe the aliens would one day reveal themselves to humanity and explain their purpose.

But then evidence began to emerge that suggested that there were some humans who knew much, much more about UFOs and aliens than was publicly available. Indeed, that they might have made direct contact with the aliens themselves. And not in the most peaceful or straightforward way.

In short, there was a UFO cover-up going on.

CHAPTER 3
CASUALTIES OF WAR

CIA director Richard Helms (right) meets US President Richard Nixon. Helms is widely believed to have orchestrated a cover-up of what the US government knew about UFOs.

Since early in the year 1950 there have been repeated rumours, supposition and some evidence that things have not gone entirely the way that the aliens controlling the UFOs would want. Indeed, some researchers suggest that things have been going wrong for the aliens right from the very earliest days of recognized UFO activity in the wake of World War II.

Many witnesses to UFO landings and the behaviour of the beings that have emerged from them reported that the aliens had seemed disturbed by the presence of humans. Whatever the aliens had landed to do, and very often this seemed to include studying wildlife and plants, had been stopped by the arrival of humans. In itself this indicated that the alien project – whatever it was – was being routinely disturbed.

That need not mean that the aliens had been deflected from their purpose. After all, they may well have built into their plans the assumption that some landings would be disturbed and cut short.

However, the loss of a UFO with its crew, and their capture by human authorities, would most certainly represent a blow to the aliens and their work. Whatever else can be said about UFOs and their crews, the desire to remain anonymous and unproven would seem to be paramount. After all, if the UFOnauts wanted to make direct and open contact with humanity, they need only land in Central Park, outside the Tower of London or in Red Square. That they choose to land in remote rural areas and flee when seen by humans must show that they wish to remain elusive.

And yet there have been repeated suggestions that UFOs have crashed, that their crews have been killed and that both UFO and crew have been recovered by human governments to be taken away for study. For obvious reasons, such allegations remain unproven. If they are true, the governments concerned have clear and pressing motives for denying that they ever happened and for covering up the evidence. If they did not take place, those same governments would have equally obvious motives for saying that they did not take place.

To find the truth, it is clear that little value can be placed on official documents willingly issued by the authorities. CIA director Richard Helms was once asked what the single most important rule of keeping secrets was. He replied, 'Put nothing on paper.' It must be assumed that if UFOs have crashed and been recovered that governments would follow Helms' advice as closely as they could.

'Although the early reports were creating a sensation in some areas and among some sections of society, others had not heard of the phenomenon or if they had, took no interest.'

There is a danger when investigating such claims, with their overtones of cover-up and conspiracy, that the researcher may come to believe in the truth of an alleged event even if the evidence does not support it. The absence of documents might be taken to mean not that the event did not take place, but that the government is covering up the truth. It is a difficult task to investigate alleged cover-ups and still keep a sense of proportion. The best that can be achieved is to look at the available evidence supporting the suggestion that UFOs have crashed and been retrieved and then try to draw meaningful conclusions from this.

The most famous and best researched such case is the Roswell Crash of 1947, but it is not the only one. Some researchers believe that the evidence for Roswell is not, in fact, the most persuasive. In any case it is probably worth taking a step back to look at other alleged crashes and the circumstances surrounding them before embarking on a study of the Roswell Crash.

Several of the reports go back to the later 1940s, so it is important to bear in mind that this was a time when people's attitudes were rather different from those of today. For a start the whole subject of UFOs, or flying saucers as they were then called, was new. Although the early reports were creating a sensation in some areas and among some sections of society, others had not heard of the phenomenon or if they had, took no interest. Even those who were interested were not yet thinking in terms of aliens. The strange craft might be Soviet missiles, secretive experiments by reclusive billionaires or some bizarre natural phenomenon. Nobody knew and few had any clear ideas. The saucers were a weird and unexplained puzzle – nothing more.

Another key fact to bear in mind is that in the later 1940s, most people were much more inclined to trust governmental authorities than they are today. The world had just emerged from the horrors and stresses of World War II. During that war everyone in the Allied countries had worked together to support their governments to defeat the Nazi regime and the expansionist might of Japan. People were accustomed to seeing the government as working for the common good. If the government wanted something kept secret, the general view was that they would have a very good reason for doing so.

A boat tows a log across Puget Sound where, in 1947, a UFO was seen apparently in serious trouble.

Public faith in government authority had not then been eroded by years of spin-doctoring and exposures of dishonesty and fraud at high levels.

The first of these cases to emerge in public came in July 1947 when Raymond Palmer, a Chicago publisher specializing in the unusual and supernatural, received a letter from a man named Harold Dahl. With the letter were a few small pieces of odd, slightly metallic material.

DAHL SIGHTING

Dahl lived on Maury Island, near Tacoma in Washington State, and earned a living locating and salvaging logs and other timber lost by the various tree felling companies working the inland forests. These logs came floating down the rivers and bobbed about in the sea until found by men such as Dahl.

According to Dahl he had been out on Puget Sound with his son and dog on 21 June when six large, doughnut-shaped craft came flying low overhead. Each craft was, he said, about 100 ft (30 m) across and coloured a dull metallic silver. One of the craft was flying erratically, dipping and lurching as it gradually lost altitude. The others seemed to be circling it protectively. Dahl whipped out his camera and took a few shots of the craft.

There then came the sound of an explosion or rumble from the stricken ship. A stream of what seemed to be molten metal erupted from the side of it and splashed hissing into the sea. The gushing material then turned darker and, apparently, heavier. Some of the material fell across Dahl's boat, causing burning and damage to the vessel and killing the dog.

The damaged craft then took off at speed. It headed west over the Pacific and disappeared from sight, pursued by the others. Dahl then doused the smouldering wreckage on his boat and headed hurriedly for home.

The following day, he was getting ready for work when a man in a dark business suit knocked on his door. The man claimed to be from a timber company wanting to discuss business and invited Dahl to a diner for breakfast. At the diner, Dahl was tucking in to his meal when the man suddenly announced that he was not from a timber business, but had come to discuss the flying saucers. He outlined the encounter even though Dahl had as yet not told anyone about it. The man warned Dahl to keep quiet and tell nobody about what had happened. He then left.

Dahl thought about the strange experience for some time, then went to see a man he knew named Fred Crisman. Dahl claimed that it was Crisman who had suggested that he contact Palmer, though events would later show this to be uncertain. Whatever the truth, events moved fast once Dahl had contacted Palmer. Scenting a good story, Palmer turned to the only man he knew who had any real experience of flying saucers – Kenneth Arnold, who had made the

Publisher Ray Palmer, who sent Kenneth Arnold to investigate the Maury Island Incident after receiving Dahl's letter.

key first report of 'flying saucers' on 24 June. Palmer paid Arnold $200 to investigate Dahl's claims next time he was in the area on business.

On 29 July Arnold flew to Tacoma, found Dahl in the phone book and called him up. That evening the two men met and Dahl showed Arnold some fragments that he claimed were solidified chunks of the material that fell on his boat. Arnold thought they looked like metallic rock of some sort. Next day, Arnold met with both Dahl and Crisman, and was shown more fragments of material. Arnold asked to see the photos that Dahl had taken, but Crisman said that they had been unable to find the camera. They would look for it again now that an investigator was on the case.

At this point Arnold began to grow suspicious, thinking that he was being strung along. He also thought that the fragments of material he was shown by Crisman and Dahl together were very different from those he had seen the night before. The new pieces looked like lava, while those he had seen earlier had been altogether stranger. Arnold called in a friend of his, A.J. Smith, for his opinion. Smith arrived that evening, and the pair agreed to meet Crisman and Dahl the next day.

That evening, Arnold had a disturbing phone call from reporter Ted Morello of the United Press Agency (UPA) who Arnold had met to discuss his own sighting. Morello told Arnold that a man had just phoned him to tell him about Arnold's investigation and to pass on verbatim conversations between Arnold and Smith in the privacy of their shared hotel room. Clearly the room was bugged, but it was not clear who by, or why they had phoned Morello.

Next day, 31 July, Smith and Arnold had their meeting with Crisman and Dahl, who handed over more fragments, but claimed still to be unable to find the camera. After the meeting, Smith agreed with Arnold that something was very fishy about the whole business but neither man could agree what. They decided to turn the matter over to the military and called Arnold's contact, Captain William Davidson

of the intelligence department of 4th Air Force HQ at Hamilton Field, California. Davidson flew up on the following day in a B25 transport along with Lieutenant Frank Brown, a fellow intelligence officer, as co-pilot. Davidson and Brown met with Crisman but not Dahl, who had gone back to work, and took possession of a box of fragments alleged to have come from the UFO. Just after Davidson and Brown left to return to the airport, Morello phoned again to say that his mysterious informant had just called to give him full details of the meeting.

' Soon after take-off, the port engine caught fire and continued to burn for some minutes before the aircraft crashed, killing both men and destroying the box of fragments.'

That afternoon, Brown and Davidson took off from Tacoma airfield in their B25. Soon after take-off, the port engine caught fire and continued to burn for some minutes before the aircraft crashed, killing both men and destroying the box of fragments. A third crew member baled out safely.

Morello then called Arnold and advised him to leave Tacoma immediately, but to check his own plane carefully first. The UPA's usual military sources had gone silent when asked about the aircraft crash and had refused to answer any questions. Not only that, but Crisman had been arrested by military personnel and bundled on to an aircraft along with his UFO fragments to be flown to Alaska. Arnold tried to contact Crisman, only to be told that he had been called away on urgent business and would be gone for several days.

Then a Major Sander of army intelligence arrived and confiscated all the alleged UFO fragments that Arnold had in his possession. Sander claimed that the whole story was a hoax and that the fragments were nothing but worthless slag from a blast furnace. He said that the pieces would be analyzed and the results sent to Arnold. Arnold never received the analysis report. About a week later Palmer's office in Chicago suffered a burglary. The only objects stolen were the fragments sent to him by Dahl along with the original letter.

FBI INVESTIGATION

In mid-August the FBI announced that they had been investigating the case. They had decided that the story had been made up by Dahl and Crisman in an attempt to cash in on the flying saucer excitement by selling interviews to press and radio. The crash that killed Davidson and Brown was an accident. No mention was made of the bugging of Arnold's room or the burglary in Chicago.

At the time, Arnold and all other early UFO investigators accepted the FBI report at face value. The FBI was the leading criminal investigation organization in the USA at the time, with massive resources to call upon and no obvious reason to mislead the public.

What neither Arnold nor anyone else looking into the Maury Island Incident knew at the time was that during the recently ended war, Crisman had worked for the Office of Strategic Services (OSS), the

'The FBI was the leading criminal investigation organization in the USA at the time, with massive resources to call upon and no obvious reason to mislead the public.'

forerunner of the better known CIA. Crisman's work for the OSS was shady and poorly documented. He may have undertaken the spreading of rumours in enemy-occupied territory, but this is uncertain.

Crisman's involvement is, all agree, central to the mystery of what really happened at Maury Island. Sceptics argue that Crisman invented the story and persuaded Dahl to act as the front man. The two men planned to make money by selling their story – just as the FBI said.

Others believe that Dahl really did have a genuine UFO experience and, not sure what to make of it, went to see Crisman because of his links to the world of spying and secret works. Under this scenario, Crisman advised Dahl to go to a private publisher because he knew that the government was not to be trusted in such matters. Alternatively some claim that Crisman was still working for the CIA and was manipulating events throughout to discredit Dahl's genuine sighting.

Arnold later went on record as saying that it had been Crisman that he distrusted all along. Dahl had struck him as an honest, though not particularly intelligent, working man who had seen something very odd that he wanted explained to him. After the FBI report came out, Dahl refused to talk about the UFO for many years. Just before his death in 1982 he broke his silence, claiming that his sighting had been real and had taken place just as he said.

With hindsight there are all sorts of unanswered questions relating to the Maury Island Incident. The involvement of an OSS operative throughout is odd — and those who harbour suspicions about the CIA would say it was downright sinister. The fact that Arnold's room was bugged again hints at involvement

Kenneth Arnold was sent to investigate the Maury Island Incident, but found his work blocked by mysterious men who may have been working for the FBI.

'Just before Dahl's death in 1982 he broke his silence, claiming that his sighting had been real and had taken place just as he said.'

by the security services. Arnold thought that the alleged debris from the saucer changed its nature as soon as Crisman appeared on the scene. Why neither Brown nor Davidson managed to get a distress call sent out from their doomed aircraft when it remained flying for some minutes after the engine caught fire

has never been explained. Nor is it obvious why that mysterious third crew member could bale out safely, but neither Brown nor Davidson could do so.

Whatever really went on at Maury Island, and subsequently during Arnold's visit, it is clear that the real truth has never come out. The event did, however, set a pattern for later incidents. An effective cover-up was orchestrated and, if it had not been for Arnold, the event might even now be virtually unknown to UFO researchers.

According to the earliest versions of the Aztec Crash, investigators gained access to the wrecked UFO through a window.

WRECKAGE IN NEW MEXICO

Another early case that was written off as a hoax and subsequently largely lost to UFO researchers was the Aztec Crash. As with the Maury Island Incident, there has recently been renewed interest in the Aztec Crash by researchers less willing to accept statements from official sources than were researchers at the time.

The story first became public in March 1950 when a man named Silas Newton gave a lecture at the University of Denver. Newton was in the oil business and claimed to have got his information from a man he called 'Dr Gee' (a pseudonym), a scientist who had been called in by the USAF to help them study a crashed flying saucer.

The report was picked up by Frank Scully, a well-respected newspaper columnist. Scully spent some time interviewing Newton, 'Gee' and other witnesses

to produce a book entitled *Behind the Flying Saucers,* published later that year. Scully later claimed that he had interviewed eight of the men who had been involved in the recovery of the crashed saucer, and had used the cover name of Dr Gee to hide their identities. The fact that he chose not to divulge the names of his sources devalued Scully's story in the eyes of some. Others thought that the need to keep secret the names of the witnesses merely emphasized the likely hostile reaction of the US government to the facts being published.

According to Scully's version of events, the crash had taken place at Hart Canyon, near Aztec in New Mexico in March 1948. The saucer was tracked on military radar as it came streaking down from the sky to impact in a remote area of near desert. At this point, the military did not know what had come down and sent out a squad to have a look. They reported back that the crashed object was a silver-coloured disc of great size that was lying intact. The military then sealed off the area from the public and put together a team of scientists and technicians who were sent out to Hart Canyon.

The initial examination of the saucer showed it to be 99.99 ft (30.48 m) in diameter. The skin of the saucer was composed of a completely smooth sheet of silvery metal with no signs of any rivets, welding or other joints. Set into the hull were a number of

> **'The skin of the saucer was composed of a completely smooth sheet of silvery metal with no signs of any rivets, welding or other joints.'**

transparent portholes, which fused directly into the silver metal without a join. There was no sign of a door, so technicians tried drilling into the metal with diamond-tipped industrial drills. They had no effect. Neither did blow torches or other tools.

Then one of the investigatory team spotted a tiny hole in one of the portholes. A thin rod was worked through the hole and used to prod a number of levers and buttons that could be seen inside. When one lever was pushed it caused a previously hidden hatchway to spring open.

Warily the team clambered into the saucer. They found that the craft was entirely undamaged apart from the small hole in the window, but that the crew of sixteen humanoids were all dead. The 3-feet (1 m) tall figures all appeared to have been charred or burned. It was theorized that some object had perforated the window, and that this had somehow killed the crew. Whether the hole had been created in airless space or within the Earth's atmosphere was unclear. The bodies were taken away for further examination.

There then followed a detailed study of the craft. It turned out to have a central section about 18 ft (5.5 m) in diameter which contained the crew's control rooms, sleeping quarters and other chambers. The outer areas of the saucer could not be accessed at first, though it seemed that they were free to rotate around the central section. After some days of fiddling and prodding, the investigators managed to dismantle the outer ring of the saucer, which transpired to be composed of a number of sections that fitted closely together.

The various pieces of the ship were then transported by road to Wright-Patterson Air Force Base for further study. Wright-Patterson, near Dayton in Ohio, was and remains to this day a top security military base where new equipment is tested under conditions of the utmost secrecy. It is also the base where captured Soviet weaponry and equipment was taken to be studied during the Cold War, so it would have been the natural place for a crashed saucer to be studied.

One of the scientists handed over to Scully a few pieces of metal recovered from the saucer. Scully had them subjected to a string of scientific tests, but apart from revealing that the pieces were composed of a complex alloy of metals, some of which could not be identified, the tests revealed nothing.

Scully's claims caused something of a sensation. Even researchers such as Donald Keyhoe, who was inclined to dismiss the story as a hoax, began to take an interest. The book based on the Aztec Crash was selling well, when suddenly the story fell apart.

A man named Leo Gebauer was arrested for fraud. Gebauer had set up a company to explore for oil and had persuaded several wealthy men to invest thousands of dollars each. The company claimed to have a device that could detect oil and other minerals through thousands of feet of solid rock. The device, it was said, had been stolen from the saucer crash at Aztec by one of the scientists who had been called in to investigate the alien technology.

The sensationalist cover of Frank Scully's book about the Aztec Crash featured scantily clad women, which rather undermined the claims of sober scientific inquiry contained within the book.

'Even researchers such as Donald Keyhoe, who was inclined to dismiss the story as a hoax, began to take an interest.'

Police were called in when one of the investors became suspicious. Investigations soon proved that the 'alien technology' was nothing more than perfectly normal mining gear put together in unusual ways. It was quite incapable of detecting oil in an oilcan, never mind through miles of rock. Police then discovered links from Gebauer to Newton, who was also arrested for his part in the swindle. At the trial, Gebauer was named as 'Dr Gee'. Both men were convicted of fraud.

Scully and all other UFO researchers rushed to distance themselves from the two conmen. Sceptics used the case to undermine the whole subject of flying saucers, claiming that Gebauer and Newton were the tip of the iceberg and that while they had been caught out the other saucer hoaxers had merely been luckier. The attacks by sceptics drawing on the alleged Aztec Crash did much to discredit the early UFO researchers and the other incidents that they sought to highlight.

Scully, however, continued to maintain that he had interviewed eight scientists involved in the study of the saucer, none of whom had been Gebauer. Moreover, it is worth noting that Gebauer and Newton had been convicted of perpetrating a fraud based on a false claim to have obtained equipment from the crashed saucer. Whether or not the saucer had ever existed played no part in the trial or their crime.

Some forty years later, investigators William Stinman and Scott Ramsey independently decided to go back to Scully's original claims to see if they could find any corroborating evidence. Between them they have turned up some interesting facts and witnesses.

Over a hundred people who had been living in the area at the time of the alleged crash were interviewed. Most could not recall anything of any interest, but four could. One man remembered that he had seen a UFO flying low overhead, but could not recall the date or even the year when it had occurred. His description of a large silver disc with a few windows matched that given by Scully. Intriguingly the witness said that the craft appeared to be in trouble, wobbling in flight and sending out sparks. He last saw it diving down in the direction of Hart Canyon. The man said that he phoned a nearby USAF base to report an aircraft in trouble, but never heard any more about it.

Two other witnesses recalled being sent out to fight a brushfire north of Aztec, near Hart Canyon, in the spring of 1948. Subsequent investigations revealed that this major fire took place on 25 March.

'Both witnesses recalled that the gangs of men fighting the fire reported seeing what looked like an unusual crashed aircraft on the ground ...'

Both witnesses recalled that the gangs of men fighting the fire reported seeing what looked like an unusual crashed aircraft on the ground, again in the direction of Hart Canyon. One of the witnesses, Doug Nolan, said that he had walked towards the object and was convinced that it was disc-shaped.

A final witness was Fred Reed, a retired operative for the OSS, later the CIA. He said that he had been sent to a location near Aztec sometime in 1948, and was in charge of a team with orders to clear up a site. He had orders to pick up any metal fragments, remove any tyre tracks that remained and to do his best to make the area look undisturbed. He said the site had been accessed by way of a newly laid gravel track and that a large concrete pad had stood nearby. The track and pad are both still there, though they are much overgrown.

Several people recalled a story about a flying saucer appearing in the local newspaper, the *Aztec Hustler*, at about the time of the alleged crash, but memories varied as to what the story had said. A contemporary account from the Aztec area printed before Newman delivered his lecture would have proved invaluable. However the *Aztec Hustler* was bought out by a larger newspaper a few years after the alleged crash and all archive copies were burned.

'... Gebauer may have invented the supposed oil locator to take dishonest advantage of the genuine story of a crashed saucer.'

It is difficult to know what to make of the Aztec Crash. Were it not for the witnesses who came forward in the 1990s, the evidence would point to the fact that the entire story had been invented by the two conmen and fed to Scully as a way to provide useful background to their claims to have obtained alien technology. On the other hand, Gebauer may have invented the supposed oil locator to take dishonest advantage of the genuine story of a crashed saucer.

The stories told by the witnesses would seem to indicate that something large and unusual came down in the approximate area of the alleged saucer crash. However, the statements were made more than forty years after the event. Most witnesses could not recall the year to which their recollections dated. Perhaps they were all talking about 25 March 1948, perhaps not. At this distance in time it is impossible to say.

SAUCER CRASHES

Another event that surfaced about this time was the Paradise Valley Crash, alleged to have taken place in October 1947. The details of this alleged event are even sketchier than those relating to the Aztec Crash. Allegedly a saucer about 36 ft (11 m) in diameter came down in the Cave Creek region of Paradise Valley, Arizona. There were two alien bodies recovered from this craft, which was in rather worse condition than that said to have been recovered at Aztec. One body was sitting upright at the controls; the second was slumped halfway out of a hatchway.

The only witness to the Paradise Valley Crash willing to give evidence openly was Selman Graves, a teenager in 1947. He recalled that some time in October he and some friends had set off on a rabbit shooting trip to Cave Creek, but had been turned back by military guards. A large area of ground was, according to Graves, sealed off. He and his friends went off hunting elsewhere, but being curious, he climbed a hill that would give him a good view of the cordoned area. Graves recalled seeing men moving about on foot, trucks traversing the dirt road that led through the area and an odd object he could not properly identify. At the time he had thought the object to be a silvery-coloured tent or dome structure and had assumed it to be something military. Only with hindsight did he wonder if the round, domed, silvery object had been a crashed saucer.

Yet another alleged saucer crash was that reported to have taken place near Laredo, Texas, on 7 July 1948. On that date a UFO was seen flying over Albuquerque at very high speed. Later that day personnel from nearby Carswell air base were mobilized to cordon off and mount armed guard over an area of barren semi-desert near Laredo. The men were told that nobody was allowed access to the area, and that they were not allowed inside the perimeter that they were guarding either. A USAF colonel went out to the site, but was denied admission by an intelligence officer despite the fact that he had high security clearance. The men guarding the perimeter of the area became convinced that they were protecting a crashed flying saucer. None of those willing to talk on the record after the event had actually seen the saucer, but they were convinced that at least one of their comrades had done.

A mysterious event that took place on 29 May 1947 has also been claimed to have been a saucer crash, though details of the incident have long been confused by the fact that they took place straddling the US–Mexican border.

At 7.20 pm the US military test-fired an experimental rocket from the White Sands range in New Mexico. It was fitted with an explosive warhead carrying a proximity fuse designed to explode when it got close to any large metallic object. The idea was that it could be shot towards fast-moving jets, exploding with enough force to bring them down without the need to actually hit them. As a precaution all aircraft were warned to stay clear of the test area.

'Five minutes later the pilot of a private light plane ... reported seeing something flying south at enormous speed and burning with a fierce, bright light.'

A short time after the missile was fired, the warhead exploded at an altitude of over 40,000 ft (12,000 m) as if it had come close to an aircraft.

Five minutes later the pilot of a private light plane some miles to the south over Juarez, Mexico reported seeing something flying south at enormous speed and burning with a fierce, bright light. A short time after that something struck the ground south of Juarez and exploded with a massive blast. Houses for miles around were shaken by the bang and hundreds of people saw a column of smoke and flames rising into the air from the impact site.

Those first on the scene found a crater about 50 ft (15 m) across and 20 ft (6 m) deep. Scrub in the area had been set on fire or singed, while fragments of what looked like sand fused to glass by intense heat

The UFO seen over White Sands, a USAF base used for testing top-secret aircraft.

were scattered all around. The Mexican military quickly arrived on the site and sealed off the area.

The USAF announced that a standard V2 test rocket, of the type acquired from Germany at the close of World War II, had gone astray during a launch. The guidance system on the rocket had, purportedly, malfunctioned causing it to head south to Juarez.

Unfortunately for the USAF, among the civilians who watched the rocket launch that day was the editor of the local newspaper. He printed a story giving details of the duration of the flight, its direction and what

happened that contradicted the abilities of a standard V2 rocket. The USAF was later forced to amend its story. Intriguingly, the editor also reported seeing a round, brilliantly lit flying object high in the sky and close to the rocket at the time when it exploded.

UFO researchers have theorized that this object was a UFO, whose presence close to the rocket caused the proximity fuse to set off the warhead. It is further conjectured that the UFO was damaged so badly that it went out of control and headed south to impact and explode outside Juarez.

In 1952 a team of top USAF intelligence officers travelled to Paris, France, to liaise with European officials on matters of high security. It has long been surmised that this conference involved discussions about UFOs. A recent verbal statement by one of the men involved says that, among other things, the crash of a UFO near El Paso, Texas, was discussed.

One of the craft tested at White Sands as part of NASA's space programme. The similarity to some reported UFOs is clear.

UNCONFIRMED EVIDENCE

There are several other stories printed in the press during the later 1940s and early 1950s that have yet to be followed up in detail by modern researchers. Typical is the Spitzbergen Crash of June 1952.

The incident began when a flight of six Norwegian military jets was on patrol over the Arctic Hinlopen Straits north of the Norwegian mainland. Quite suddenly the jets' radios were swamped by static as they crossed the coast of the island of Spitzbergen. The flight commander, Captain Olaf Larsen, ordered his formation to circle while he tried to reach base on his radio. He failed, but far below him he caught a glint of sun sparkling off metal. Going down to investigate, Larsen saw what he took to be a large, circular metal object embedded in the snow of the remote frozen island. The craft was said to be around 150 ft (45 m) in diameter and bore abstract symbols of some kind.

When Larsen and his men got back to base they reported their find to the Norwegian Air Force. Thinking that the object might be a secret Soviet missile that had gone off course, the Norwegians sent a search team to inspect it.

No further press reports were ever printed. Whether this was because the object turned out to be something utterly mundane or because the Norwegian government imposed a news blackout is unknown.

Similarly, reports of a crashed saucer in Germany came to nothing. This UFO was reported to have been discovered wallowing in the shallows off the coast of the island of Heligoland. The object was a disc about 90 ft (27 m) across and made of a silvery metallic fabric. The authorities were alerted, and sent a team of scientists to investigate. The press then reported that the metal skin of the craft withstood temperatures of 15,000 degrees without melting or buckling and that the bodies of seven humanoids could be seen inside.

As with the Spitzbergen Crash, the press fell suddenly silent on the Heligoland Crash. There were no follow-up reports. Either the truth turned out not to be newsworthy or the press were persuaded not to print anything further. It is well known that some newspapers and magazines – though not the more respectable ones – are prone to recycling good stories. It is a possibility, but no more than that, that these one-off stories of crashed saucers in the later 1940s and early 1950s were put together by an editor to liven up an otherwise dull issue on a 'slow news day'. The story of the Aztec Crash would be the most likely origin for such a deception.

One case that was most definitely not a recycled story and which occurred rather later than the others took place in Wales late on the night of 23 January 1974. The initial reports of something odd taking place made the national news headlines, both in newspapers and on television. As so often, however, the authorities made determined efforts to downplay the event. Only later did the train of events become clear, and even then it was never entirely certain what they meant.

EERIE LUMINESCENCE

It all began around 6.30 pm when several people in Cheshire, England, called the police and reported seeing a large glowing disc slipping silently overhead. Some reported seeing three flying objects, but all agreed that what they had seen had emitted a pale green glow of eerie luminescence.

Two hours later, at just past 8.30 pm, a massive blast shook the village of Llandrillo in Wales. The entire population of the village felt and heard the explosion. Objects were knocked off shelves and pictures tumbled from walls. Pouring out into the street, the villagers saw a blaze of lights coming from high up on the Cader Berwyn mountains to the east. The glow varied from green to blue to orange, arcing high into the sky, then dying down only to flare up again. Then came another rumble as a second blast shook the area.

A pair of local policemen were on the scene quickly. After discussing the matter with witnesses, they concluded that an aircraft had crashed on the mountainside. They radioed back to their headquarters to request support. Borrowing an off-road vehicle from a farmer, the policemen drove up an unmade road to get on to the mountain. They soon discovered that their access was blocked by broken ground, but they could see glowing lights a mile or so away.

Meanwhile, a second team of police had roused the local district nurse, named Pat Evans, and asked her to accompany them to the site of a suspected aircraft crash in case she could be of help to any injured survivors. Evans and her escort made their way up on to the hills by way of a different route and managed

The first men up on the mountains above Llandrillo, Wales, on 23 January 1974, saw a large glowing object resting on the ground.

to get to within striking distance of the crash site before having to abandon their vehicle.

Walking over the broken mountain pastures, Evans and the police soon realized that what they could see was not the normal burning wreckage of a crashed light aircraft, as they had been expecting. The lights were not flames or smouldering wreckage, but seemed to be some sort of electrical glow that pulsated, changing shade and intensity. At a distance of about 200 ft (60 m) away, Evans and the policemen halted. The glow could now be seen to be coming from an oval or rounded object that seemed to be intact, resting lightly on the turf. Unsure what to do, they kept their distance and watched.

Soon afterwards some Royal Air Force (RAF) men arrived. They said that they had orders to clear the area so that a team of RAF investigators could examine the crash and the wreckage. Evans and the policemen were escorted from the mountainside. By dawn the next day the mountain had been sealed off by the RAF, and remained closed to the public for several days.

When the locals were once again allowed back up on to the mountain, the area was empty. It was as if nothing had ever happened. There was no debris, no crater, no wreckage.

Several days later the authorities announced that there had been no aircraft crash after all. The loud explosion had, in fact, been an earthquake that struck the area. The shaking of houses could certainly be

'By dawn the next day the mountain had been sealed off by the RAF, and remained closed to the public for several days.'

explained by a tremor, as could the two distinct roars as if an explosion had taken place. However, the lights seen dancing on top of the hills by dozens of villagers were more difficult to account for.

Some people have reported seeing what are called 'earth lights' during earthquakes. These appear similar to the aurora seen near the poles, but do not seem to be either as bright or as long-lived as the lights seen at Llandrillo. In any case, there is no firm scientific explanation for earth lights so to explain events in terms of earth lights merely replaces one mystery with another. And even earth lights could not possibly explain the object seen by Nurse Evans.

Many people believe that a UFO fell to earth at Llandrillo that night. Whether it subsequently flew off again, or was captured by the RAF, is unknown.

The majority of these stories of crashed UFOs being retrieved for study by military authorities date to the period 1947 to 1953. And yet of all the places that got their names into the media or came to the attention of UFO researchers, there is one that is glaringly obvious by its omission. It is a name that now dominates discussion of aliens and UFOs, but at the time was not even discussed.

That name is Roswell.

THE ROSWELL CRASH

In the past few years, the Roswell Crash has taken on almost iconic status among both believers and sceptics in the realms of UFO research. For believers it is a case that holds out the tantalizing prospect of actually proving that not only do UFOs exist, but that they are piloted by aliens. For sceptics, the Roswell Crash offers the chance to disprove a key event and so, by implication, debunk the whole subject of UFOs and dismiss them from serious consideration.

It is the mysterious nature of the events that took place at Roswell in July 1947 and the peculiar way in which they have come out into the public domain that has excited both sides of the debate. Allegations of subterfuge, cover-up, conspiracy and more have been thrown around. For all that, it is important both to try to stick to the known facts and to bear in mind what was going on both at the time of the event and in more recent years when witnesses who had remained silent for decades chose to come forward with their stories.

Although the Roswell Crash was largely overshadowed by other news at the time, it did receive a small amount of media attention. That was sparked by a press release issued by Lieutenant Walter Haut of the public relations department of Roswell air base at 11 am on 8 July.

That original document has since been lost, but the Press Agency (PA) report based on it has survived. It went out at 2.26 pm Roswell time and reads:

> ### 'It is the mysterious nature of the events that took place at Roswell in July 1947 and the peculiar way in which they have come out into the public domain that has excited both sides of the debate.'

Roswell, NM. The army air force here today announced a flying disc had been found on a ranch near Roswell and is in army possession. The Intelligence office reports that it gained possession of the disc through the cooperation of a Roswell rancher and Sheriff George Wilson of Roswell. The disc landed on a ranch near Roswell sometime last week. Not having phone facilities, the rancher, whose name has not yet been obtained, stored the disc until such time as he was able to contact the Roswell sheriff's office. The sheriff's office in turn notified a major of the 509th Intelligence Office. Action was taken immediately and the disc was picked up at the rancher's home and taken to the Roswell Air Base. Following examination, the disc was flown by intelligence officers in a superfortress (B29) to an undisclosed Higher Headquarters. The airbase has refused to give details of construction of the disc or its appearance. Residents near the ranch on which the disc was found reported seeing a strange blue light several days ago, about three o'clock in the morning.

The sheriff's name was actually Wilcox, but otherwise this report accurately reported what most people who saw the original press release recall.

The '509th' referred to was the 509th Bomb Group of the USAF, which was based at Roswell. This group was a touchy subject with the USAF. It was a force of heavy, long-range bombers that were capable of carrying atomic bombs. Indeed, it was the only force of bombers in the world that had atomic bombs on base and ready to be used. The aircraft could not reach the Soviet Union from Roswell, but facilities were in place at refuelling points to allow them to get into Soviet air space within 15 hours of a war breaking out. The sensitivity of the USAF to anything involving the 509th needs to be borne in mind.

Similarly, there were many who felt that if the UFO aliens were worried about humanity's use of atomic power then the 509th at Roswell was bound to be a key target for their surveillance.

A few minutes later, the PA sent out an update naming the 509th intelligence officer who was handling the case as Captain Jesse A. Marcel. A later update stated that Lieutenant General Hoyt Vandenberg, deputy chief of the army air forces, was handling the USAF comment on the story from his office in Washington DC.

Although the report said merely that Marcel was handling the case, his role was much greater than that. It was Marcel who had collected the wreckage from the ranch, driven it in a truck to Roswell and was now escorting the crates of material to the airfield at Fort Worth.

NEWSPAPER STORY

In Fort Worth, Texas, a reporter named Bond Johnson of the *Fort Worth Star* got the AP report. He knew that transport aircraft from Roswell usually came to the Fort Worth air base to be transferred through the depot facilities there. He called General Roger Ramey, who confirmed that the wreckage from Roswell was coming to Fort Worth, and then set off for the air base.

On arrival at 4.30 pm, Johnson was shown quickly to Ramey's office, which was unusual as he normally met his contact in the press room. Ramey's office was strewn with small pieces of debris. There were balsa wood struts, pieces of charred rubber and aluminium foil sheets. Ramey told Johnson that this was the 'saucer wreckage' flown in from Roswell, and

'Similarly, there were many who felt that if the UFO aliens were worried about humanity's use of atomic power then the 509th at Roswell was bound to be a key target for their surveillance.'

then shattered Johnson's hopes of a major story by identifying the debris as a crashed weather balloon. Johnson photographed the material and trailed back to his office.

Meanwhile, the USAF in Washington had issued a press release saying that the wreckage was being taken to Wright-Patterson airfield for study.

At 5 pm, Johnson finished developing his photos

The site of the alleged Roswell Crash, which lies amid semi-desert scrub near the town in New Mexico.

of the debris shown to him by Ramey and began transmitting them out over the AP wire service. By this time the Roswell phone system was jammed. Neither the air base nor the sheriff's office could make any outgoing calls due to the vast number of calls flooding in. Others were able to make local calls, but all lines out of the town were busy.

Ramey called a press conference which was attended by all available local reporters and a live radio link provided by NBC. It was now 6.15 pm. Ramey told the assembled newsmen that the 'flying saucer' was no such thing, then handed over to the Fort Worth meteorological officer, Irving Newton. Newton displayed the wreckage, identifying it as

Retired USAF officer Jesse Marcel handled some of the Roswell wreckage and in 1978 went public with the story of a UFO crash.

parts of a rain target balloon and pointing out the key identifying features. The newsmen were convinced.

At 6.31 pm the news went out over the AP service that the 'saucer' was a crashed weather balloon. Interest in the story collapsed and died. Only a few newspapers and radio stations had covered the Roswell event before the story was effectively killed by Ramey.

One man, however, was not content. Major Jesse Marcel was convinced that the debris shown by Ramey to Johnson and displayed at the press conference was not the same debris that he had brought from Roswell by aircraft. He knew what a weather balloon looked like, even after it had crashed, and while he agreed that the debris as displayed was

a balloon he was convinced that the debris he had brought with him was not.

Marcel was, however, a busy professional USAF officer with a career to think about. If the authorities wanted to keep the truth secret, he suspected that they had good reasons for doing so. As the months and years passed, however, he began to wonder about what had really happened and became somewhat unsettled by the continuing official silence. He began to talk about his experiences to friends.

SURFACING EVIDENCE

In 1978, UFO researcher Stanton Friedman was in Baton Rouge doing a broadcast when he heard by chance that a local man claimed to have handled wreckage from a crashed saucer. By this date the Roswell story had been forgotten by the UFO research

> 'At 6.31 pm the news went out over the AP service that the "saucer" was a crashed weather balloon. Interest in the story collapsed and died.'

community, so the claim came as something of a shock to Friedman. He did, however, recognize the importance of the story, so he took the time to locate and interview the man – retired Major Jesse Marcel.

Marcel told Friedman what he knew, which, although suggestive of both a genuine crashed

The front page story that first broke the news of the Roswell crash in 1947, before the story was quashed by the military.

saucer and a widespread government cover-up, fell far short of actual proof. It was, after all, the unsupported word of a retired military officer getting on in years.

The world of UFO research was very different in 1978 from how it had been in 1947. There were more people involved with the research, operating with more funds and better facilities. The idea that UFOs were piloted by aliens was by 1978 more widely accepted than it had been in the later 1940s, when Soviet Russia was still thought to be a credible source of the objects.

Crucially, the researchers were less willing to accept official statements and explanations at face value. There was a widespread and growing conviction that the authorities, and the US government in particular, knew far more about UFOs than they cared to admit.

With this new background to UFO research, Friedman went to work on Marcel's claims. He was soon joined by others and within a few years the truth behind the events at Roswell began to surface. It is fair to point out that only some of what has emerged can be categorized as facts that are accepted as such by all concerned. Other details rest on the memories of people speaking decades after the event. While there is no reason to suspect these people of lying, they are trying to recount things that occurred long before and it is possible that dates, times and other details have become blurred, confused or forgotten. And there is always the possibility that a few witnesses have simply made up their accounts out of a misplaced sense of humour or for unknown reasons of their own.

DEBRIS FIELD

That said, what seems to have happened at Roswell is this. On the night of 4 July 1947 a rancher named Mac Brazel heard what he took to be an explosion take place over the Foster Ranch where he was working as

'The wreckage consisted of hundreds of pieces of lightweight metal, short beams made of some sort of plastic, metal foil and a string-like material.'

foreman. Riding out next day he found an area of rough pasture scattered with small pieces of wreckage – this would later become known as the debris field. The wreckage consisted of hundreds of pieces of lightweight metal, short beams made of some sort of plastic, metal foil and a string-like material. Brazel collected a few pieces, which puzzled

him very much. He was unable to cut them with his knife, or burn them with a match despite the fact that they appeared to be very thin and flimsy.

On 6 July Brazel went into town and reported his find to Sheriff Wilcox. Wilcox sent a pair of deputies out to take a look. Then, thinking that the debris must have come from an aircraft, he called Roswell air base in case they knew anything about the incident. It was then that Captain Jesse Marcel was sent out with two other men to investigate. After calling on Wilcox, Marcel drove out to the Foster Ranch. It was now getting dark, so he decided to return the next morning.

Early on 7 July Marcel was shown the debris field by Brazel. Marcel recalled that the wreckage was scattered over an area about 75 yd (68 m) wide and 800 yd (730 m) long. There was a deep gouge in the earth in the centre of the area as if some heavy object had struck the ground and then flown off again.

Marcel and his men spent most of that day collecting the pieces of wreckage. One vanload of debris was sent off to Roswell air base in the early afternoon and Marcel drove the second load himself as dusk was closing in. Both Marcel and Brazel kept a few pieces of wreckage, showing them to friends and relatives who all recalled its strange properties. The foil would spring back to its original flat condition if screwed up in the hand, the struts could not be cut and none of it could be burned.

On the following morning, Marcel and base commander Colonel William Blanchard studied the

Colonel William Blanchard, the USAF officer who authorized the press release announcing a UFO crash at Roswell.

As Friedman and others continued their research, they began talking to others who had lived in Roswell or served on the air base at the time. Their recollections soon indicated that something much more dramatic than some debris falling to earth had taken place.

Much of this testimony was suggestive of something odd going on, but did not provide a clear idea of what. Many people said that areas of the air base were sealed off for several days by armed guards. Others recalled the arrival and departure of aircraft carrying senior officers, and that the flights were kept secret. Some civilians remembered that air force personnel had sealed off a fairly large area of land north of Roswell for some days. This was not the Foster Ranch, but an area several miles away. Everything pointed to the fact that something important and unusual had happened.

pieces of wreckage. It was after this that Blanchard ordered Haut to issue the press release that sparked off the media interest.

Marcel then loaded the crates of debris into an aircraft and flew with them to Fort Worth. There he handed them over to Ramey, who opened the boxes and pulled out several pieces of wreckage. Marcel then left to eat and refresh himself. When he returned to Ramey's office, Marcel recalled, the debris had all been removed and replaced with the torn up pieces of a weather balloon that were shown to the press.

'There was a deep gouge in the earth in the centre of the area as if some heavy object had struck the ground and then flown off again.'

Then two witnesses came forward to describe a UFO. James Ragsdale and William Woody both said that they had seen a bluish-white UFO streak overhead north of Roswell and appear to crash into the ground. Others later also recalled seeing this object, but they could not be certain of the precise date.

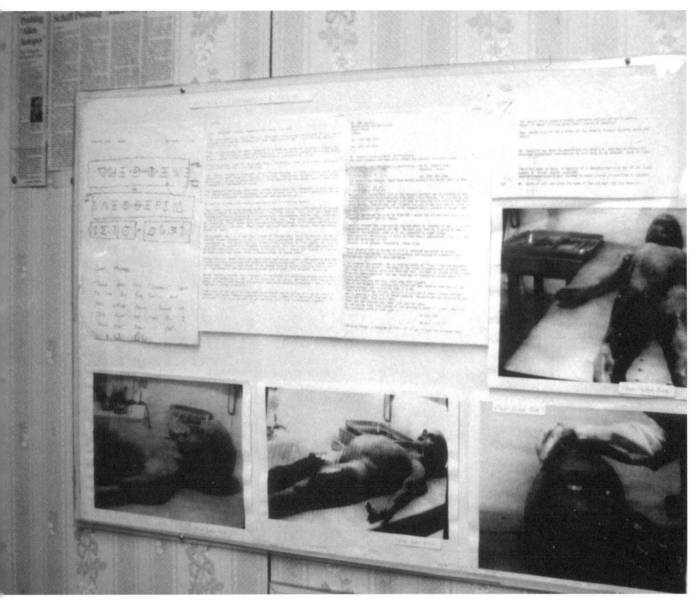

Photos at the Roswell UFO Museum that purport to be stills from the autopsy on the alien bodies recovered from the crash.

HUMANOID BODIES

Several people came forward to say that a man named Barney Barnett had seen a crashed aircraft in the sealed-off area, and that he had seen three diminutive humanoid bodies in or close to the crashed object. Barnett had found the object early on the morning of 5 July. As he looked at it he was joined by a group of archaeologists. Then a squad of USAF men arrived and escorted them all away from the site. Unfortunately Barnett himself had died in the intervening years, but his account seemed to have been consistent whenever he told it.

Researchers tried to track down the archaeologists. The task took some years, complicated by the fact that the men had not been archaeologists but anthropologists. Finally the team leader was found. Dr Curry Holden was aged 92 by the time researchers reached him, and was easily confused. He could remember no dates and the details he gave were contradictory and rambling. Nevertheless he was clear that he had been near Roswell and had seen a crashed aircraft of a type he could not identify.

Other witnesses included Glenn Dennis, who worked in the mortuary in Roswell. He recalled that at the time of the incident, he had been contacted several times by staff at Roswell air base asking him how to preserve bodies in the desert heat. This was unusual as on the few occasions when someone had died on the base, Dennis had been called out to care for the body. This time he was barred from dealing with the body himself. At the time he had formed the opinion that somebody important had died, or been killed in an accident, and that the USAF did not want word to leak out.

Many others recalled conversations with personnel from the air base that indicated that strange, inhuman bodies had been found and were being subjected to an autopsy.

Perhaps the clearest evidence to emerge is not that relating to a crashed UFO or its crew, but to the desperate attempts by the USAF to cover up what was going on.

Brazel was arrested and kept under armed guard for several days after he reported his finds. He was then frogmarched by his guards to talk to reporters with the specific message that he had been mistaken in his earlier comments that the debris had been unusual. He was then ordered to keep silent as the matter touched national security. As a loyal American, he stayed quiet.

'Brazel was arrested and kept under armed guard for several days after he reported his finds.'

Some years later Brazel's son Mac found a few odd pieces of the debris at the family house. He told some friends and within days USAF officers called and impounded the pieces.

VEILED THREAT

Frank Joyce was working at the Roswell radio station. He remembered getting an official call from Washington DC telling him that the station's licence to broadcast would be revoked if they continued to cover the story.

Finally there is the official story as put out by Ramey and the USAF. This was that what Brazel had found was nothing more than the wreckage of a weather balloon. No mention was made of the alleged crash site north of Roswell. As we have already seen, the weather balloon explanation has been put out by the authorities several times to explain sightings, even when it was patently untrue. Both the West Malling Incident and the Gorman Dogfight were explained away in this fashion. The explanation has been used too often for it to have any inherent credibility.

SPY BALLOON

When the researchers began to turn up new evidence that contradicted the official story, the USAF at first made no comment. Then, in 1995, they issued a new report that claimed to be the result of exhaustive internal investigations. This report said that the original story about a weather balloon had been entirely false. It had been issued to cover up the truth, that the debris found by Brazel had been the wreckage of a Mogul spy balloon that, in 1947, had been top secret.

According to this account, the wreckage came from Mogul Launch No.4. This balloon disappeared from radar scopes over New Mexico in mid June. The security clampdown imposed at the time, the USAF said in 1995, was designed to protect Mogul from public view.

Researchers soon found problems with the new report. The Mogul balloons certainly carried top

> **'... the debris found by Brazel had been the wreckage of a Mogul spy balloon that, in 1947, had been top secret.'**

secret, high-tech equipment but the balloons themselves were little different from standard weather balloons. The components did not match the descriptions of the debris given by Brazel, Marcel and others.

Nor were other Moguls treated with the same degree of secrecy as the events at Roswell. Mogul

The materials of the Mogul balloon (seen here) were unlike those described by the people who handled the Roswell wreckage.

Launch No.6 went off course and crashed. It was found by a farmer named Sid West who at once identified it as a USAF balloon and called the air force to come and collect it.

Again, the USAF has used this changing explanation before. They had at first said that Gorman had been chasing a weather balloon. When this was conclusively disproved, they changed the explanation to identify the UFO as a military high-altitude helium balloon.

In any case, the new explanation still ignored the growing though largely circumstantial evidence of the recovery of dead bodies. Two years later the USAF issued another report. This one did address the issue of recovered bodies. It said that the bodies were probably crash test dummies used by the USAF to measure the injuries likely to be caused to the human body by a variety of air accidents and events. No evidence was offered that such tests had taken place around Roswell.

> ## 'Certainly something crashed, certainly it was taken away for study by the USAF and certainly the authorities went to a great amount of trouble to try to keep the affair secret.'

Even with the benefit of hindsight it is impossible to know what happened at Roswell. Certainly something crashed, certainly it was taken away for study by the USAF and certainly the authorities went to a great amount of trouble to try to keep the affair secret. If nothing else the Roswell investigations served to increase the certainty among many researchers that the USAF knew far more about UFOs than it was letting on.

Whatever the truth of the various crash stories and reports, there are some features of the tales that hint at some wider conspiracy or plot. One such was a feature of the Maury Island Incident that was entirely overlooked at the time and only appeared to be significant as the years passed: Harold Dahl's

mysterious breakfast caller. According to Dahl this man was dressed in a dark business suit and claimed to be a timber merchant. At first his behaviour matched his claims, but he then recounted to Dahl the details of the UFO encounter, details that nobody could possibly know, and went on to utter threats with the aim of forcing Dahl to remain silent. These threats were unspecific, but decidedly menacing. Interestingly, once Dahl went public the man did not return and his threats came to nothing.

These traits would later become well known to researchers investigating UFO incidents. Time after time witnesses were visited by similar, sinister and threatening men. They came to be known as Men in Black, or MiB. Most MiB encounters followed the pattern set by the man who visited Dahl.

MIB ENCOUNTERS

Another early case took place in 1952 after an Italian named Carlo Rossi saw a UFO while fishing on a secluded stretch of river near San Pietro a Vico. It was not his usual fishing spot and it was some weeks before he returned. Within minutes of setting up on the river bank, Rossi was approached by a man

> ## 'The man then offered Rossi a cigarette and suggested they have a quiet chat. Rossi accepted the cigarette, but as soon as he began smoking it he began to feel unwell.'

Will Smith and Tommy Lee Jones dressed as Men In Black for the Hollywood movie of that name. The film was a comic take on the rather more sinister activities of the real life MiB.

dressed in a dark blue business suit. The man spoke with what Rossi thought to be a Scandinavian accent and had a very pointed nose. The man asked Rossi if he had seen any odd flying objects in the area recently. Rossi said that he had not. The man then offered Rossi a cigarette and suggested they have a quiet chat. Rossi accepted the cigarette, but as soon as he began smoking it he began to feel unwell. The stranger apologized, took the cigarette back and tore it up. Then, without another word, he left.

In May 1964 a British fireman named James Templeton found what looked like a man in a spacesuit in one of the photos he had taken during a day out in Cumbria. He had not noticed the figure at the time, but it was quite clear on the photo. Two men in dark suits arrived the next day in a black Jaguar car and knocked on his door.

> **'He had not noticed the figure at the time, but it was quite clear on the photo. Two men in dark suits arrived the next day in a black Jaguar car and knocked on his door.'**

The men said that they were from the government and had been sent to investigate the spaceman sighting. They asked Templeton to accompany them to the site of the incident, five miles away, and drove him there in their car. Once on the spot, the men asked a variety of questions that baffled Templeton – about the weather at the time and the behaviour of wild birds in the area, for instance. After a while the men turned angry. They stormed off, jumped in their car and drove off. Templeton had to walk home.

In 1967 a man named Robert Richardson accidentally crashed his car into a landed UFO near Whitehouse, Ohio. Next day he discovered a few pieces of odd, lightweight metal attached to his car. He reported the find to the local police and to UFO research group Aerial Phenomena Research Organization (APRO), run by Coral and Jim Lorenzen. Later that evening two young men pulled up at Richardson's house in a black 1953 Cadillac carrying the licence plate 8577-D. The two men knocked on Richardson's door and engaged him in a friendly but rather pointless and inconsequential conversation for a few minutes. Then they left.

A week later, two different men called on Richardson. These men wore dark business suits and had swarthy complexions. One of them spoke with a strong accent, and Richardson concluded that they were foreign. At first the two men sought to persuade Richardson that he had not seen a UFO at all, still less hit one. When that failed they asked for the pieces of metal. Richardson refused, saying that he had already posted them off to APRO.

The two men then turned nasty and adopted a threatening manner. 'If you want your wife to stay as pretty as she is,' one of them sneered, 'you had better get the metal back.' Then they left. Richardson saw

> **'At first the two men sought to persuade Richardson that he had not seen a UFO at all, still less hit one. When that failed they asked for the pieces of metal.'**

them walk down the street, climb into a 1967 Dodge and drive off. He did not get the licence plate this time.

Alarmed, Richardson contacted APRO and had them check the licence plate of the Cadillac. The licence plate had never been issued. As so often, Richardson never saw the men again and their threats proved to be empty.

It is not only UFO witnesses who receive visits from MiB. Researchers do as well. In October 1975, investigator Herbert Hopkins received a phone call from a man claiming to be interested in a recent case that Hopkins was handling and asking if he could drop by to discuss it. He agreed. Less than a minute later the man was on the doorstep. This alone puzzled Hopkins. This was in the days before mobile phones and no public phone box was in the vicinity.

The man was dressed in a black business suit, which looked a bit old-fashioned to Hopkins, and was totally bald. He did not spend much time discussing the particular case he had mentioned, but instead engaged the researcher in general chat about UFOs.

The mysterious intruder then asked Hopkins to hold a coin on the palm of his hand. As Hopkins watched the coin first turned blue, and then vanished from sight. The visitor said: 'Neither you nor anyone else on this planet will see that coin again.' He then asked Hopkins if he knew how one UFO witness had died. Hopkins did, the man had died of a stroke. 'No,' replied the man, 'he died because he had no heart, just as you no longer have your coin.'

Suddenly the visitor stood up. 'I must go,' he said. 'My energy is running low.' He walked straight to the door and let himself out. Then he walked away into the night.

The MiB usually claim to be from the government, police or some other official agency, though they will sometimes purport to be journalists or even UFO researchers. When these claims are subsequently investigated, they turn out to be false. The ID cards or other forms of documentation that the MiB show their victims, on the other hand, either are genuine or very good forgeries.

Exactly who the MiB might be and what they hope to achieve has long been a problem for UFO researchers. The men usually appear to be perfectly normal human beings — the Hopkins encounter was very untypical. They dress smartly in dark colours and when their vehicle is seen it is always a perfectly

> **'The mysterious intruder then asked Hopkins to hold a coin on the palm of his hand. As Hopkins watched the coin first turned blue, and then vanished from sight.'**

The typical MiB will arrive as if from nowhere, and leave just as mysteriously.

normal car — though usually large, dark and sometimes rather old. Their behaviour usually runs along a set pattern. They talk to the witness or researcher in general terms and with a friendly manner before moving on to ask specific questions about a sighting. These questions often appear to focus on apparently inconsequential details. The MiB then seek to convince their victim to keep quiet or to accept a mundane explanation for the incident. If the witness refuses, the MiB become angry and make threats. Then they leave.

At first researchers assumed that MiB were government officials seeking to intimidate witnesses into silence. The fact that their claimed identities

turned out to be false suggested that the agencies involved did not want to be linked to the intimidation of civilians.

However, other researchers have focused on the odder aspects of the case. As the term Men in Black suggests, the MiB are usually dressed in dark business suits and arrive in dark cars. They have strong accents and speak as if conversing in a foreign language. Some, such as the one met by Herbert

'The MiB then seek to convince their victim to keep quiet or to accept a mundane explanation for the incident. If the witness refuses, the MiB become angry and make threats.'

'It has been suggested that the MiB are aliens pretending to be humans, or that they are robots sent by aliens.'

Hopkins, behave very oddly. It has been suggested that the MiB are aliens pretending to be humans, or that they are robots sent by aliens.

If the MiB are accepted as aliens, theirs are not the only purported conversations held between humans and aliens. Though conversations with MiB are typically inconsequential, frightening and soon over, the same cannot be said of those who claim to have had prolonged and repeated contact with the aliens who pilot UFOs.

CHAPTER 4
ALIEN CONTACTS

O n 20 November 1952 the owner of a hamburger restaurant at Paloma came staggering out of the Californian desert to tell the world that he had not only seen a UFO and its occupants, but had spoken to them as well. The man's name was George Adamski and his claims would revolutionize the study of UFOs.

Before that fateful day in 1952, Adamski had led what might be politely called a colourful life. He had been born in Poland in 1891, emigrating to the USA with his family at the age of two. In 1913 he joined the US Army, riding with a cavalry unit that patrolled the Mexican border during the volatile years of the Mexican Revolution and subsequent civil wars.

By the later 1920s, Adamski was living in Laguna Beach, California, where he founded a mystical religious sect that he called the Royal Order of Tibet. Adamski announced that a vital part of the religious ceremonies of his new sect involved imbibing small amounts of alcohol. On the strength of this he was granted a licence allowing him to produce wine, even though Prohibition was in force at the time. A fair amount of the 'sacred wine' found its way on to the black market and Adamski earned a good living.

When Prohibition ended, Adamski and his disciples began to take their religion more seriously. They recruited a number of followers impressed by the spiritual aspect of the sect. One of the new recruits was persuaded to buy a farm near Palomar Mountain, while others donated cash to the movement. At

One of the photos produced by George Adamski of what he claimed was a scout ship from the planet Venus.

Palomar, Adamski set up a restaurant and he was running this establishment at the time of his interplanetary encounter.

According to Adamski, he had seen several UFOs in the Palomar region from 1943 onwards. In 1950 he took a grainy photo of what he claimed was a UFO. The photo and an article Adamski had written were published in *Fate* magazine. Adamski made contact with other early UFO researchers, sharing information and ideas. Among the ideas that Adamski put forward was that the UFOs favoured certain places and regions for navigational purposes, which was why they were seen over these places more often than others.

In 1952 he began visiting the places that he had identified as likely to be visited by a UFO. Friends asked if they could come along, and Adamski was happy to take them with him. On one such trip to Desert City, California, Adamski was accompanied by two couples, Mr and Mrs Al Bailey and Mr and Mrs George Williamson.

CIGAR-SHAPED OBJECT

According to the account given by the five people, they were scanning the skies when they saw a large cigar-shaped object swooping silently down towards them. The object came down to hover a few hundred feet above the ground and some thousand or so yards away. Adamski set off on foot across the desert to investigate, while the others stayed where they were.

Adamski came to within 200 yd (180 m) of the object when a small saucer-shaped craft detached itself from the UFO and came down to circle him before flying back to the mother ship. Adamski took a photo of the circular craft, which he dubbed a Scout Ship.

Then Adamski noticed a man standing about 400 yd (360 m) away who had not been there before the Scout Ship flew past. Adamski walked over to the man who turned out to be very human in appearance. The man was about 5 feet 6 inches (1.7 m) tall, of average weight, and looked to be in his twenties. He had blond hair falling to his shoulders, green eyes and a slight suntan. The man was dressed in a brown overall, which was fairly tight and appeared to be all of one piece without any obvious fastenings. He wore sandals on his feet.

Adamski at once assumed that this very human-looking figure was an occupant of the UFO. Adamski tried talking to the alien, but could not apparently be understood. Then he tried sign language and facial gestures. This provoked more of a response. Then the man touched his arm in a particular way (Adamski never revealed how), and suddenly the two were conversing by means of telepathy.

> 'Adamski tried talking to the alien, but could not apparently be understood. Then he tried sign language and facial gestures. This provoked more of a response.'

According to Adamski the alien's name was Orthon, and he came from the planet Venus. Orthon said that beings from other planets within the solar system, and from beyond, were also visiting Earth. The purpose for the visits was to warn humanity about the dangers of nuclear power and other aspects of technology then being explored by scientists. Orthon said that the Venusians had decided against public contact with Earth's assorted political leaders as they feared a violent reaction. Instead they had opted to maintain surveillance on humanity's progress and to contact a few select individuals – of which Adamski was one.

Alien Contacts

An artist's impression of Orthon, the alien that George Adamski claimed visited him numerous times in the 1950s.

Adamski then asked Orthon if he could take a photo of the Venusian and his craft to prove the experience to others. Orthon refused, but offered to take a roll of film away with him. The Scout Ship then returned, Orthon entered and it flew off. Adamski returned to his friends.

Together they walked back to the site of the encounter to inspect the footprints left by Orthon. These seemed to be real enough, and Adamski cast them in plaster of Paris. As the five humans walked back to their car, they saw a military jet swoop low over the area, then a second arrived and together the two aircraft criss-crossed the desert as if carrying out a search for something.

Adamski claimed that a few weeks later he felt an urge to return to the site of the encounter. The Scout Ship appeared once more, but Orthon did not emerge. Instead a small object fell from the UFO. Adamski hurried to pick it up, finding that it was the roll of film he had handed to Orthon. When developed, the film was covered in a mass of symbols and hieroglyphs that Adamski was unable to decipher. Nobody else has ever been able to make sense of them either.

As with his earlier sightings and ideas, Adamski circulated details of his encounter with Orthon to his fellow researchers and other interested parties. One of these was the British writer Desmond Leslie who was working on a book about flying saucers. Leslie asked Adamski to write out a full and detailed account of the meeting with Orthon for him to include as an appendix to his book. Adamski obliged. When he got Leslie's manuscript, the publisher promptly made Adamski's account the central feature both of the book and of the publicity material.

BEST-SELLER

The book came out with the title *The Flying Saucers Have Landed,* and proved to be an immediate best-seller in Britain. When it came out in the USA a few months later the book caused a sensation. Researchers lined up to take sides in the disputes

Desmond Leslie (left) and George Adamski working on the manuscript of one of their books about Adamski's experiences.

that followed. Some hailed Adamski as a man who had made genuine contact with the aliens when nobody else had managed to do so. Others denounced him as a fake.

Adamski himself became the centre of a media scrum as interviews were demanded, magazine articles commissioned and profiles published. Inevitably, pressure built from the book publishers for a sequel. In 1955, Adamski and Leslie obliged by delivering the manuscript for the book *Inside the Space Ships,* released in the USA as *Inside the Flying Saucers.* The book made claims even more astonishing than those relating to the encounter of 20 November 1952.

The book opened with an account of a visit Adamski made to Los Angeles on business in February 1953. Having completed his meetings, Adamski was approached in the street by two men. One touched his arm in the same way as Orthon had done and again communication became possible. The two men led Adamski to a car and began driving him out of the city. They explained that one was a Martian named Firkon, the other was named Ramu and was from Saturn and that they were taking him to meet Orthon.

Orthon led Adamski into a Scout Ship, which took off and docked with a much larger spaceship high in the stratosphere. Throughout his telling of this encounter, Adamski gave highly detailed and circumstantial accounts of what happened. On entering the mother ship he was escorted to a doorway.

'As I stepped through the doorway,' Adamski wrote, 'into a luxurious lounge, my attention instantly was absorbed by two incredibly lovely young women who arose from one of the divans and came toward us as we entered.' He went on to give detailed descriptions of the two stunning aliens, how one had long blonde hair and 'golden eyes that held an expression that was both gentle and merry', while the other had long black hair and black eyes with flashes of brown. Both were, Adamski said, 'an image of perfect beauty'.

The book ran to almost 200 pages of such material. The saucers and other spaceships were described in great detail, though technical data was vague and virtually meaningless. The account detailed how the aliens spoke at length to Adamski about the horrors of war, the futility of human existence and the superior aspects of their own Space Brotherhood. The messages were endowed with a good deal of portentous language and symbolic imagery, but could be condensed down to a plea for humans to be nice to each other for a change.

'Adamski was approached in the street by two men. One touched his arm in the same way as Orthon had done and again communication became possible.'

Again the book sold in huge numbers and Adamski made a good deal of money. Over the years that followed, Adamski produced a number of other books, a number of photos of UFOs and a continuing if frustratingly vague stream of messages from the aliens begging humanity to behave itself. Adamski claimed to have travelled to the Moon and to Saturn on board UFOs.

By 1960, public interest in Adamski and his tales had flagged. Not only was there a complete lack of any sort of proof to back up his stories, but the rapidly increasing scientific knowledge of our solar system was refuting many of his claims. It was discovered, for instance, that the surface of Venus is so hot that lead would melt. An essentially human creature such as Orthon could not possibly live there.

Adamski died in 1965 and the truth of his claims and stories died with him. That has not stopped some researchers from trying to discover what had been going on. That Adamski's later claims and books were mostly science fiction is not in serious doubt. Nor can there be much doubt that Adamski was the sort of man who would spot a good opportunity to make money and cash in on it to the maximum.

That does not rule out the possibility that his first encounter with Orthon was, at least to some degree, genuine. Adamski made no wild claims about that meeting, other than that he had met and communicated with an alien. He did not claim to have entered a saucer, still less to have flown to the Moon. Nor did Adamski, at least at first, seek to make money out of the meeting. Instead he contacted other researchers seeking their ideas and thoughts on the event.

It has also emerged that Adamski had some sort of contact with both the FBI and the CIA. Exactly what form this clandestine communication took has never been revealed, though it is known that in the mid 1950s CIA director Allen Dulles refused to allow a researcher to talk to any CIA staff about Adamski on the grounds of national security.

In fact, Adamski's initial experience was not so very different from those reported by others who have claimed to meet and talk to aliens. More than one researcher thinks that Adamski had a genuine experience of some kind, but later cranked up the fictional fantasy to make money. That his later claims were so obviously false did much to discredit the subject of UFOs in the eyes of many members of the public. Perhaps, it has been suggested, that was what the CIA had planned all along.

THE ALIEN PROPHET OF CARACAS

Although it sometimes seems that all alien encounters happen in America or Europe, they are a truly international phenomenon. On 7 August 1967 Dr Sanchez Vegas of Caracas, Venezuela, was visited by an alien who stood about 4 ft (1.2 m) tall and asked for a physical examination. Vegas did as requested, discovering that the creature had ten teeth, no ears and eyes that were completely round – among other things.

When Vegas asked the alien how he came to speak such perfect Spanish, the being replied that he and his fellows learned Earth languages with machines. He went on to say that on his home planet there were no wars or diseases and he did not have any parents since his race 'reproduced in a different way'. Before leaving, the alien warned Vegas that there was a deep rock fissure buried far below Caracas that was gradually filling with water. When full, it said, the fissure would burst, causing a devastating earthquake in the city.

The message of impending doom for mankind coupled with a Utopian view of the alien's own world was similar to the information given to Adamski. So was the message received by James Cook just outside Runcorn on 7 September 1957.

VISITORS FROM ZOMDIC

Cook saw a round object, pulsating with coloured lights. It came swooping down to hover a few feet above the grass, which was wet from earlier rain. A telepathic voice told Cook to jump on to a rail, but to be careful not to touch the rail and ground at the same time due to the machine's powerful electric field. Cook did as instructed and entered the UFO. He found himself in a large, empty room, illuminated by a soft glow that oozed from the walls. The voice told him to change into a one-piece suit that lay on the floor. Again, Cook did as he was told.

An artist's impression of the aliens and UFO interior as described by James Cook after his encounter of 1957.

The object then flew off to dock with a larger craft, on board which Cook found the beings who controlled both. The crew were basically human in both size and appearance, although Cook noted that they had childlike faces. The beings informed him that they came from the planet Zomdic, and that on their world there was eternal peace among the race that was neither male nor female but reproduced in a different way.

The beings from Zomdic told Cook that they had been visiting Earth for some time as they were deeply concerned for the future of humanity. The constant squabbles between groups of humans and the frequent recourse to force was upsetting the natural balance of the planet. Humans should, the Zomdicians said, try to find a more harmonious way of solving problems. They ordered him to go and tell humanity.

> **'The beings from Zomdic told Cook that they had been visiting Earth for some time as they were deeply concerned for the future of humanity.'**

Cook, displaying a sense of proportion rare in those who claim to speak to aliens, said that he doubted that the rest of humanity would believe him since he was just an ordinary working man. 'They won't believe anyone else either,' replied one Zomdician with a sense of great sadness.

Cook then returned to Runcorn the way he had come. On departing from the saucer, however, he forgot the warning about touching it and the ground at the same time and received an electric shock that badly burned his arm. Although he thought that only two or three hours had passed, Cook found that it was now two days after he had first boarded the UFO.

MARTIAN FARMERS

Broadly similar was the experience of farmer Gary Wilcox at Tioga, New York State, on 24 April 1964. He spotted a silver-coloured oval object about 25 ft (7.5 m) across lying in the corner of a field and went to investigate. As he approached he saw two men, each measuring about 4 ft (1.2 m) tall and wearing a one-piece overall outfit. They were carrying soil samples on dishes that they had taken from the field.

The figures told the astonished Wilcox that they had come from Mars and were interested in Earth agriculture. Wilcox began explaining his farming methods, prompting a string of questions from the aliens. He got the impression that the Martians were deeply unimpressed by the level of human technology. They were, however, intrigued by his descriptions of the yearly and daily cycle of life and seemed bemused by the concept of time. When he mentioned fertilizer, they asked Wilcox to get some. Wilcox strode back to his barn, but when he returned with it both the aliens and their craft had gone. He left the bag on the ground and it disappeared overnight.

One of the highly profitable UFO conventions organized by Orfeo Angelucci after his encounter with aliens in 1952. Financial gain is often said to be a motive of UFO witnesses by sceptics, but very few ever make much money.

In July 1950 Daniel Fry spotted a landed saucer in New Mexico. As he walked forward to investigate, a figure stepped out and held up a hand to stop him. 'Better not touch the hull, Pal,' said the new arrival in faultlessly modern American English. 'It is still hot.' When he made to leave in alarm, the being spoke again. 'Easy, Pal. You're among friends here.'

Fry says that he was then taken on a ride inside the saucer, zooming north-east to circle over New York City before returning to New Mexico. The round trip took a little over thirty minutes. The alien then explained that his name was A Lan and that his race of aliens were descended from beings called Lemurians who had previously lived on Earth but had fled the planet thousands of years earlier after an atomic accident of undefined type. A Lan told Fry that the aliens were visiting Earth as they were concerned that the planet's technological progress was racing

Witness Truman Bethurum claimed that the commander of the UFO he encountered was a stunningly attractive woman dressed in a velvet bodice and red skirt.

ahead of the sociological and religious developments needed to keep it under control. Then A Lan flew off, leaving Fry alone.

These one-off encounters, including Adamski's first meeting if it is considered separately from his later claims, all fit into a general pattern, along with dozens of others. The beings that claim to be aliens appear just once. They claim to be from a specific alien planet and state that they are visiting Earth for benevolent reasons. They very often show interest in aspects of life on Earth, seemingly so that they can point out differences with their own existence. Almost invariably they pass on a warning of some kind, though it is usually so vaguely worded as to be useless.

EARLY CONTACTEES

One contactee, (as people who claim to have spoken to aliens have became known), who did receive a warning of a very specific kind was Orfeo Angelucci. Angelucci was working at the Lockheed aircraft factory in California when, on 24 May 1952, he encountered a UFO. He said that the UFO came down to land. From it emerged a sort of movie screen on which were displayed two beings of indescribable beauty. After a few seconds the screen withdrew and the ship flew off.

Two months later, Angelucci again saw a UFO, this time resting on the ground near his home. The craft had an open door on its side and Angelucci stepped in. At once the door slammed shut behind him and the craft began to move. Not at all frightened, Angelucci wandered about the empty craft until he found a porthole. Looking out, he saw Earth as a distant globe.

A voice then came from some unseen source which delivered a lecture on the miserable state of humanity compared to the peace and tranquillity of more advanced civilizations. Earth, Angelucci was told, was known as the 'home of sorrow' among the space beings. The voice warned Angelucci that unless mankind got a grip on its rapidly advancing technology and used it for benevolent purposes there would take place 'The Great Accident' in 1986. This would lead to the extinction of humanity.

Returning to his home, Angelucci was so profoundly moved by his experience that he began telling friends and colleagues about it. They failed to take him seriously, but a publisher put out a book that Angelucci wrote about his contact under the title of *Secret of the Saucers*. It sold well, but subsequent works by him did not make as great an impact on the public. By the 1960s he had faded from public notice. Angelucci died in 1993, having seen his prediction of a global catastrophe in 1986 unfulfilled.

Unusual in that her contacts with aliens did not involve the sighting of any type of UFO was Cynthia Appleton. This British housewife claimed to have met an alien which materialized from thin air in her home in Birmingham on 18 November 1957. The being returned several times during the course of the following year. The messages he passed on included the statement that UFOs were visiting Earth to extract a mineral from sea water and that his people had mastered the use of gravity for power. Like Adamski's alien, the one visiting Appleton also claimed to come from Venus.

> ## 'A voice then came from some unseen source which delivered a lecture on the miserable state of humanity compared to the peace and tranquillity of more advanced civilizations.'

Another early contactee was Truman Bethurum, a highways repair man from Nevada. He claimed that he had been sleeping in his truck after coming off night shift when he woke up to find himself surrounded by a group of humanoid figures about 4 ft (1.2 m) tall. A metallic saucer-shaped object about 300 ft (90 m) in diameter hovered nearby. The humanoids gestured for Bethurum to follow them to the saucer, which he did.

Inside the saucer, Bethurum says that he was introduced to the humanoids' commander, who turned out to be a stunningly attractive and very human woman named Aura Rhames. She was dressed in a black velvet bodice, red pleated skirt, and red and black beret. Aura Rhames, Bethurum says, told him that she came from the planet of

Clarion. This planet orbited Earth, but was never seen as it was on the far side of the Moon.

Over the next three months, Bethurum met Aura Rhames eleven times. During these visits the two conversed freely in English, chatting about life on Clarion, political events on Earth and other subjects. After the eleventh visit Aura Rhames did not return.

> **'... he suddenly realized that it was a landed flying saucer and turned to run. A voice then boomed out of the object, declaring: "Do not be frightened, we are not hostile. We are not hostile. We mean you no harm."'**

One of the most detailed one-off encounters was reported by TV repairman Sid Padrick of Watsonville, California. On 30 January 1965 Padrick was driving home late one night when he saw a large, round object in a field. Approaching out of curiosity, he suddenly realized that it was a landed flying saucer and turned to run. A voice then boomed out of the object, declaring: 'Do not be frightened, we are not hostile. We are not hostile. We mean you no harm.'

Padrick stopped running and again approached, though this time more warily. A door opened in the side of the craft and Padrick was invited inside by what appeared to be a perfectly normal human male aged about 25. Padrick entered. There he was to meet a number of the aliens, one of which was a very pretty young woman.

Padrick described the aliens as being very like humans, but with a few superficial differences. Their fingers were longer and more delicate, their faces had unusually pointed noses and chins while their auburn hair looked rather odd in an undefined way. The beings were all dressed alike in one-piece outfits which included integral boots. There was a waistband and neckline decorated with patterns, but no obvious means of fastening such as buttons or zips.

Padrick was shown over the UFO, passing through a variety of rooms, each of which contained crew members working on instruments, controls and screens of various kinds. Only one of the aliens claimed to be able to speak English; the others communicated with each other via telepathy. This alien told Padrick that they came from a planet that could not be seen from Earth and that they travelled at speeds governed only by light. He was shown a photo of a city on the aliens' home world in which the buildings were mostly in the shape of domes.

The humanoid went on to describe a near-perfect society with no crime, long life expectancy, no disease and harmonious co-operation between the individuals. There was no money in circulation as all the individuals worked voluntarily and had their needs provided for. In response to a question from Padrick as to why the beings visited Earth, the alien replied: 'For observation.'

The interior of the UFO entered by Sid Padrick in 1965 was filled with sophisticated equipment of unknown purpose and design.

Padrick was then invited into a special room to say prayers to the 'Supreme Deity' before being deposited back at his truck. He hurried to report the encounter to the USAF, not realizing that he was but one in a succession of people to report similar encounters. The USAF sent an officer to question Padrick about his alien contact. After a short visit the officer seemed to lose interest and left, advising him not to discuss the matter with civilians. In particular, according to Padrick, the officer seemed keen that the public should not know that the aliens used no money or that they were friendly.

After a while without further official contact, Padrick did go public. He spoke to the press on several occasions and gave numerous interviews. In 1968, however, he announced that he would no longer speak about his experience, having said all there was to say and wanting to get on with his private life.

CLAIMS OF REGULAR ALIEN CONTACT

On another level altogether is the one-armed Swiss farmer Eduard 'Billy' Meier who claims to have been contacted by aliens on a regular basis. Meier says he

A photo taken by Meier that he claims is of the alien Semjase.

first met an alien from the Pleiades star cluster at the age of five in 1944, but that regular contact did not commence until 28 January 1975.

The encounter of 1975 was with a devastatingly beautiful female alien named Semjase. Over the next few years, Meier claimed to have met other aliens called Ptaah (the name of an Egyptian god), Quetzal (the name of an Aztec god) and Plaja, among others. These beings are said to have dictated to Meier around 3,000 pages of detailed information about science and philosophy among the stars. Meier produced a series of photographs of the Pleiadian saucers to support his claims. Opinion on the photos is divided. They are very clear and detailed, but whether they show small models close to the camera or large moving objects far from the camera is uncertain. The various experts who have studied the pictures have come to different conclusions.

During the 1980s Meier founded and ran the Semjase Silver Star Centre in Switzerland as a place where the teachings and knowledge of the Pleiadians could be passed on to humans. The centre was very successful for a while, but then public interest in his claims began to fade.

In later years, Meier claimed that the aliens had taken him back in time to meet and converse with a number of famous historical figures, including Jesus Christ. At the time of writing, Meier is predicting that a cataclysmic world war will break out in November 2011.

REALITY, HOAX OR DELUSION?

It is usual among UFO sceptics, and even among most mainstream UFO researchers, to dismiss claims made by contactees as being utter nonsense. Some believe that the claims are lies or hoaxes perpetrated to boost book sales, promote tourist attractions or merely for self publicity. Others see the claims as being made perfectly genuinely by people who do believe that they have spoken to aliens, but who in fact have been the victims of hallucinations or delusions.

Two cases, both famous in their time but now usually dismissed as hoaxes, are often cited by sceptics determined to dismiss all contactee reports as frauds.

In 1954 the book *Flying Saucer from Mars* appeared, which listed the author as Cedric

A photo taken by Billy Meier that purports to show a UFO coming in to land near his home in Switzerland.

Allingham. In the book Allingham told how he had been walking along a beach near Lossiemouth in Scotland when he saw a flying saucer swoop down low overhead. The saucer raced out to sea, then turned about to return and land on the beach close to him.

A door opened in the side of the saucer and out stepped a being that looked exactly like a human male in his early thirties. The new arrival was wearing a one-piece overall of some silvery fabric. There then followed a conversation between Allingham and the alien, during which they communicated using sign language and by drawing pictures in the sand. This culminated when the alien indicated that he came from Mars and promised to return.

Allingham found a local fisherman who had seen the saucer, and persuaded him to sign a witness statement that was then included in the book.

In the 1960s, investigators decided to track down Allingham and interview him. The publishers of the book at first said that he was out of the country, then later that he had died. No trace of a Cedric Allingham of Lossiemouth could be found and it was not long before the investigators suspected a hoax. Later findings pointed strongly to a well-known British astronomer famous for his mischievous sense of humour, but he stoutly denied that he had anything to do with the affair.

'Others see the claims as being made perfectly genuinely by people who do believe that they have spoken to aliens, but who in fact have been the victims of hallucinations or delusions.'

The second apparent hoax was the long-running UMMO affair. This began on 6 February 1966 when a UFO was seen over Aluche, a suburb of Madrid. The sighting seems to have been genuine enough, but what followed was not. A photo of the UFO was sent to the local newspaper. It showed a pale grey disc-shaped object flying overhead. On its underside was a symbol that looked rather like }+{. At the time the photo seemed to be genuine; it stood up to all the tests that the newspaper could think of and was accepted by Spanish researchers as a photo of a genuine object.

The photograph that appeared in Cedric Allingham's book and which claims to be of an alien. The book is now thought to have been a hoax.

A few weeks later a number of metal cylinders were found scattered about Madrid. Inside each cylinder was a piece of flexible material that carried the symbol)+(. The cylinders were fairly rapidly identified as being made of nickel, though of a remarkably pure kind not in general industrial use. The flexible material, however, defied analysis. It seemed to be some sort of plastic, but could not be identified. It was astonishingly tough and strong, while remaining very thin and bendy. Some hailed it as an example of alien technology.

Then Spanish UFO researcher Fernando Sesma received a packet of typewritten documents, each of which prominently carried the)+(symbol. Within months other researchers had also received similar packs. The envelopes were posted from locations all over the world and arrived in an apparently random order so that the contents of each pack made little sense until put together with documents from other envelopes. Together the collection ran to over 3,000 pages of closely typed material.

When put together, the documents claimed to have come from an alien race from the planet UMMO in the IUMMA star system, located about 14.6 light years from Earth. Much of the writing purported to be accounts of exploratory visits by beings from UMMO to Earth. These included some well-known UFO sightings as told from the point of view of the UFO pilot; others mentioned obscure reports and some related to events not known to the researchers.

The rest of the documents claimed to be scientific and mathematical works based on Ummite technology. At first they did not make much sense, but then a researcher realized that the mathematical articles referred to calculations in base 12, whereas

'Then Spanish UFO researcher Fernando Sesma received a packet of typewritten documents, each of which prominently carried the)+(symbol.'

One of the mysterious UMMO letters that it was claimed came from aliens, but have been unmasked as part of a long-running hoax.

most modern Earth calculations are in base 10. Once this was noticed, the mathematics not only made sense but included some highly advanced mathematical concepts and proofs that only a highly trained expert could have understood. The articles relating to physics seemed to be based on a concept as different from our current understanding of physics based on Einstein's work as Einstein's theories of relativity were different from the ideas of Isaac Newton.

For a while many researchers became highly excited by the UMMO affair. It was theorized that the material was a genuine attempt by extraterrestrial aliens to establish contact through recognized UFO researchers. But then the whole UMMO affair began to fall apart.

In the later 1970s new and more sophisticated methods of analyzing photos were applied to the original UFO picture. This showed it to be a small model fairly close to the camera and not, as claimed,

The photo that started the UMMO affair. It claimed to be of a UFO seen over Madrid in 1966, but was in fact of a model flying saucer.

a large UFO about 200 yd (180 m) away. Likewise the odd plastic material turned out to be Tedlar, a hi-tech covering used by NASA in the manufacture of space vehicles. When communications from UMMO stopped the whole affair was written off as a hoax.

However, some researchers were not content with this. The hoax had been highly sophisticated, and had clearly involved a huge amount of time, effort and money on the part of the hoaxer. At least one person with advanced scientific and mathematical knowledge had been involved, and so had somebody with sophisticated photographic skills. Crucially, the

hoaxer had managed to get hold of Tedlar, which in 1966 was a classified substance accessible only to NASA or other agencies. This seemed a lot of trouble to go to for a mere practical joke at the expense of UFO researchers. In any case, nobody came forward to claim the hoax and so enjoy the resulting publicity.

Some researchers began to suspect that there was more to it than a joke. It was pointed out that the CIA, USAF or other American government agency would have had access to Tedlar in 1966, but a normal prankster would not. Some began to theorize that the whole UMMO affair had been developed by government agencies with the purpose of undermining the credibility of UFO researchers to the general public. It was seen as a ploy in a continuing campaign to persuade the public that there was nothing to the UFO reports.

More darkly, some thought that the prime purpose of a hoax might have been to mislead UFO researchers and throw them off the track of what was really going on.

Despite such high-profile cases turning out to be frauds, not all researchers dismiss the contactee experience as entirely false.

INTERPLANETARY PASSION

Among the various features that seem to be consistent with these alleged contacts with aliens — that the beings are basically human, are friendly and issue warnings — it must be noted that the presence of attractive young women in the alien crew recurs time and again. This feature was taken to an entirely new level during the contact claimed by Brazilian farmer Antonio Villas Boas on 16 October 1957.

After the encounter was over, Boas contacted Dr Olvao Fontes for treatment of wounds resulting from the encounter. Fontes in turn contacted UFO researcher and journalist Joao Martinas. Martinas considered the story that Boas had to tell so exciting that he decided to keep the report secret in the hope that something similar might take place to corroborate it. Martinas also feared that if the Boas

report became public there might be a number of copycat hoaxes that would undermine the credibility of the event. It was not until 1965 that the outline of the story got in to the public domain, and full details were not released until 1969.

According to Boas the events began on the night of 5 October 1957 as he and his brother were going to bed in their remote farmhouse near Sao Francisco de Sales. The two young men saw a bright light in the farmyard. While they debated whether or not to investigate, the light rose in the air, shone through the gaps in the roof tiles and then flew off.

On 14 October the brothers were out ploughing in the cool of the late evening when a round object emitting a bright light drifted down to hover at the far end of the field. Antonio decided to investigate, but every time he got close to the object it flew off to come to rest 100 m or so away. After three attempts at reaching the object, Boas gave up and the object flew off.

The following evening, Antonio was out ploughing alone. At 1 am he saw what looked like a red star moving across the heavens. It dived down and came towards him. As Boas watched he saw that the red light was only the brightest feature of a large flying object. What he saw was oval in outline with a flat base and a revolving domed structure on top. The rim was dotted with purple lights while the bright red light took the form of a cone projecting forward from the front of it. So far as Boas could tell the main body of it

> **'He had taken only a few steps when he felt something grab his arm. Turning round, the frightened farmer saw a humanoid about 5 ft (1.5 m) tall.'**

was composed of smooth silvery metal. A bright spotlight flashed on to bathe the whole field in light as bright as day.

The craft came to a gentle halt to hover several feet above the field and about 50 ft (15 m) away from Boas. Then three leg-like structures descended from it and came to rest on the ground. The landing of the object shook Boas out of his inaction. Pushing his foot on the accelerator, he slewed his tractor around and powered towards the gate. The tractor's engine abruptly died, as did its lights. Leaping down, he began to run.

He had taken only a few steps when he felt something grab his arm. Turning round, the frightened farmer saw a humanoid about 5 ft (1.5 m) tall. Boas punched the being, which fell sprawling in the mud. Again he tried to run, but this time was brought down by three humanoids. Kicking and struggling, Boas was carried towards the craft.

Each of his assailants was dressed in a tight, one-piece grey outfit with no obvious way of fastening. The arms ended in integral gloves while the legs ended with boots which had very thick soles. On the chest was a round metal plate of a reddish colour which was linked to a thick belt by what seemed to be a strip of metal.

On the head of each alien was a cylindrical, square-topped helmet of a metallic substance. The front of the helmet had a clear panel through which peered large, pale eyes. Three tubes emerged from the top of the helmet. The central tube curved down to enter the suit halfway down the back. The other two also entered the suit, each one into an armpit.

Despite his struggles, the beings managed to carry Boas to their craft and, with some difficulty, up a ladder and into the UFO. Once inside, the door slammed shut and he was put down, though two of the aliens kept a tight hold on him. Two more beings now entered the brightly lit room where they were standing, one of whom then led the way through a door into an oval chamber that had a table and some chairs in it.

RUFF COMMUNICATION

The beings then began to talk to each other using what Boas later likened to dog barks, though he emphasized that barking was not quite accurate. He said that the sounds included barks, yelps and odd drawn-out noises quite unlike anything he had heard before and beyond his abilities to mimic.

After some minutes of this, the aliens fell silent and pounced on him. They stripped him of his clothes, and then washed him down with a clear, oily liquid that evaporated quickly from his now naked skin. He was then shepherded towards a door, over which was engraved what seemed to be red symbols of some kind. Boas memorized the symbols and later wrote them down, but they defied all attempts at translation.

In this new room, Boas was pushed to sit on a soft couch. One of the creatures then approached him holding a flask from which extended two tubes. One of these, ending in a suction cup, was affixed to his chin while one of the aliens manipulated the other. Boas was alarmed to see the flask filling up with his blood. The aliens inspected the sample closely, then walked off, leaving Boas alone.

When the door slid open again, it was to reveal a startling figure. The newcomer was a woman as naked as was Boas. The farmer was at once struck by the stunning beauty of the woman, whose attractiveness seemed to overwhelm him. Any thought that Boas had that the woman was a captive like himself were quickly scotched by her slightly odd appearance.

Although she appeared human, the woman had abnormally wide hips, a sharply pointed chin, large eyes that slanted outwards and bright red pubic hair. The woman led the farmer to the couch and soon

The disturbing encounter experienced by Antonio Boas began when he was wrestled to the ground by beings that emerged from a UFO.

made it very clear that she wanted to have sex with him. Boas found himself more than willing. When they had finished, the woman walked towards the door where she was met by one of the short aliens. The woman paused to look back at Boas. She pointed to her stomach, then to Boas, then upwards. He took this to mean that she would one day return to take him to the stars.

'They then began to take him on a tour of the UFO, but this was cut short when he picked up a strange instrument and tried to slip it into his pocket.'

The short aliens then returned Boas' clothes to him and waited while he got dressed. They then began to take him on a tour of the UFO, but this was cut short when he picked up a strange instrument and tried to slip it into his pocket. He hoped that having this tool would convince others of the reality of his bizarre experience. The aliens, however, spotted the move. They grabbed the object back amid much barking and yelping. Boas was then hustled out of the craft and pushed down the ladder to the ground.

The object retracted its legs as the purple and red lights began to pulsate. It climbed slowly into the air, then suddenly accelerated away at high speed. Boas was left alone.

Later that day a severe headache began, followed by waves of nausea and periodic vomiting. A few days

'A few days later, Boas noticed that his skin was breaking out into odd round, purple blisters that became infected and painful.'

later, Boas noticed that his skin was breaking out into odd round, purple blisters that became infected and painful. His eyes puffed up and became very sore and sensitive to bright lights. After contacting his own doctor, Boas was directed to Dr Fontes for study. Fontes thought that Boas might have been suffering from some form of radiation sickness, but could not be certain. The symptoms cleared up within a few weeks. Joao Martinas, meanwhile, subjected the farmer to a succession of detailed interviews and cross-examinations designed to catch him out on details or to otherwise discredit the story. But Boas remained consistent throughout. Martinas concluded that he was telling the truth. Boas later declined to give interviews, preferring to get on with his life. He did, however, continue to insist on the truth of his encounter up to his death in 1988.

At the time, the Boas Incident was put down as a very unusual and somewhat menacing contactee experience. With hindsight, however, it was seen to have much in common with a form of alien encounter that was to become disturbingly familiar. Hundreds of people have since claimed to have been abducted by aliens for a series of bizarre, painful and deeply sinister reasons.

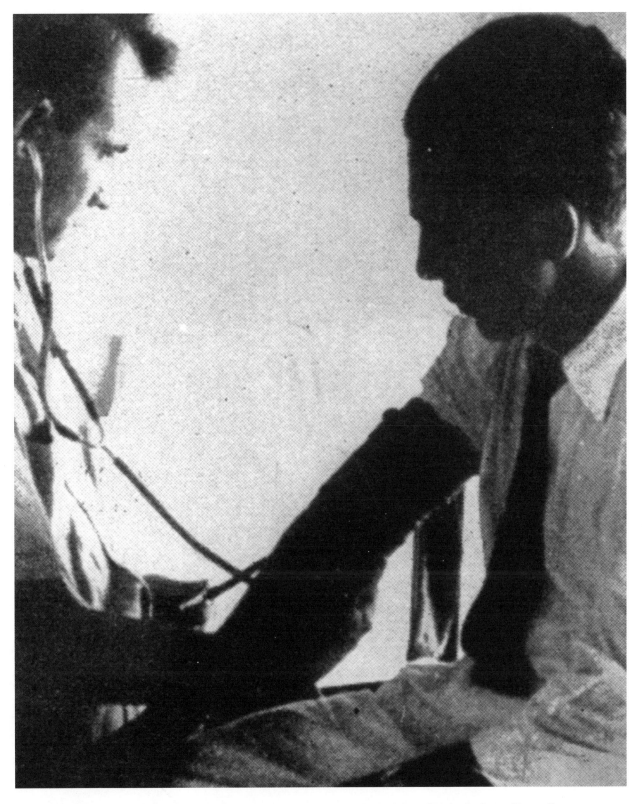

Boas undergoes medical tests as part of the investigation into his extraordinary claims of having had sex with an alien woman.

CHAPTER 5
HUMAN HARVEST

Most alien abductions begin when a UFO is encountered and the witness is approached by humanoids.

For over ten years after the initial Kenneth Arnold sighting of 1947, UFO researchers tried to work out what the UFOs were and what their purpose was. It was gradually accepted by mainstream investigators that UFOs were highly advanced technological machines, almost certainly from another planet, and that they were crewed by beings with a deep interest in humanity.

At first the contactee experiences of George Adamski and others seemed to offer a solution to the UFO mystery. But as the number of contactees grew, and the points of agreement between their tales became fewer, that hope faded. Researchers began to look around for other sources of explanation, with more than a few beginning to suspect that the authorities, and in particular the US government, were covering up the truth.

Then a case came to light that seemed to offer a new perspective on the whole UFO experience – and a disturbing one at that. At first the encounter stood alone as a unique event, but soon it was joined by many others.

ALIEN ABDUCTION AND THE 'MISSING TIME' EPISODE

The story of the abduction of Betty and Barney Hill has become one of the great classics of the UFO story. It is worth retelling not only as it is interesting in itself, but to highlight a few points that are sometimes ignored by those more keen on the sensational aspects of the encounter.

On the evening of 19 September 1961 Barney and Betty Hill set off home from a holiday in Canada to Portsmouth, New Hampshire. They expected to arrive

Betty and Barney Hill undergo hypnotic regression as part of the investigation into their encounter with a UFO and its alien crew.

home around 3 am. The long night drive passed without incident until the couple were south of Lancaster, New Hampshire. Then Betty spotted a bright white light in the sky that looked like a large star, but which was tracking them.

Barney, who was driving, pulled over to have a look. He thought it was an aeroplane, and using the binoculars he kept handy in the car, he climbed out for a better view. Through the binoculars he saw that the flying object had no wings, but was large and dark with a row of windows through which peered a number of humanoid faces. The creatures seemed to be taking a deep interest in the Hills.

Suddenly frightened, Barney leapt back in the car, fired up the engine and raced off. There followed some strange beeping noises coming from behind the car, which sounded out twice. Then the UFO was gone and the Hills were motoring home. They arrived

at around 5 am, two hours later than they expected and neither could account for the delay.

And that, so far as the Hills were concerned, was that – at least at first. As the study of UFOs stood at the time the sighting of humanoids inside a UFO would make this an interesting incident in itself but it would have been unlikely to make any headlines. In any case, the Hills did not report the encounter.

A week later, Betty began to suffer from intensely vivid nightmares. Although the details varied, they all centred on Betty being kidnapped and subjected to painful procedures by short humanoids. About the same time, Barney suffered from painful stomach ulcers. Wondering if there was any link to the UFO sighting, the Hills contacted researchers, who were the first to spot the discrepancy between the expected and actual arrival time of the Hills.

The researchers suggested that the Hills get in

touch with Dr Benjamin Simon, a psychiatrist who would be able to explore any deep-seated emotional trauma caused by the sighting that might account for the nightmares and ulcers. It was Simon who hit upon the idea of using hypnotic regression to explore the missing two hours of time to see if this revealed anything of relevance.

The tale that came out was consistent between the two Hills, disturbing in its content and unsettling in its implications. Although the emotional responses of both Betty and Barney were so great under hypnosis that it took several attempts and careful questioning to draw out exactly what had happened, the final story was clear.

The 'missing time' episode began when Barney got back in the car after seeing the humanoids through his binoculars. The car would not restart, and soon a group of the aliens had emerged from the UFO and were surrounding the vehicle.

The humanoids were slightly shorter than humans, being around 5 ft (1.5 m) tall. They had pale grey skin and large black eyes that wrapped around the sides of their heads. Their noses were short and snubbed while their mouths were small and slit-like with narrow blue lips. The figures were dressed in black one-piece suits and several of them wore black cap-like headgear.

The figures opened the car doors and dragged the couple out. At this point Barney fainted. Betty said that he seemed groggy throughout the experience

A drawing of one of the aliens that abducted the Hills, based on Betty's description.

that followed, while Barney was able to recall only occasional details. The couple were dragged on board the UFO and led into separate rooms.

Barney could not recall what happened to him other than that he had been laid on a table and examined, but Betty could recall more detail. She said that the aliens took fingernail clippings, hair samples and a scrape of skin from her arm. She then had a long needle inserted into her stomach, a procedure which caused her intense pain. One of the aliens, who was taller than the others, bent over her and waved his arms over her head, at which point the pain subsided. This alien, who Betty thought must be a leader, then spoke to her, saying that they were carrying out a pregnancy test.

The examination over, Betty and the lead alien had quite a long conversation. She thought that they had been talking telepathically, but was not certain. The alien asked Betty about a variety of mundane things, such as how vegetables were used, before Betty ventured to ask where the aliens were from. The lead alien showed her a star map with their home system clearly marked on it. Neither Earth nor the Sun were on the map, so Betty said it was not much use to her. The alien replied, 'If you don't know where you are, there is no point in my showing you where I am from.'

Betty then asked for something that would prove to other humans that the encounter had really taken place. The leader handed over a book, that Betty opened to see was filled with symbols of some kind. At this point several of the smaller aliens came forward to object, but the leader ignored them.

Betty Hill in later life when she became a regular speaker on the UFO circuit.

> 'The lead alien showed her a star map with their home system clearly marked on it. Neither Earth nor the Sun were on the map ...'

Barney then rejoined Betty. The aliens leading him in had his false teeth in their hands. They asked Betty what they were and wanted to know if her teeth came out as well. After this, the aliens led the Hills out of the UFO and back towards their car. Suddenly the lead alien reappeared and told Betty that he had decided not to let her keep the book. Nor would the Hills be able to remember what had happened. They were then put back in their car and the UFO took off. It was at that point that the 'missing time' ended. Barney started the engine and raced off.

Under hypnosis, Betty drew a copy of the star map. This was studied by a number of astronomers, who put the data through sophisticated computer modelling software. Although not everyone who has studied the results agrees, many astronomers think that it shows the Zeta Reticuli system.

Zeta Reticuli is a two-star cluster about 37 light years from Earth. The two stars are about the same size and brightness as our own Sun and seem to be about 8 billion years old, only slightly older than our Sun. Although they are too far away for a planet to be detected, they are of the correct type of star to have planets orbiting in the crucial zone where carbon-based life forms could exist.

This seemed to offer some supporting evidence for the idea that the UFO crew were aliens, especially as Betty Hill had no knowledge of astronomy and would have been unlikely to be able to create such a map on her own. On the other hand, it does seem a bit odd that aliens capable of interstellar travel should need something as basic as a map. Even in 1969 the US astronauts travelling to the Moon did not use a map, but computerized telemetry. Some researchers thought that the map was used as the aliens thought that Betty might understand it, others that it was a false lead concocted by the UFO crew to convince Betty of something that was not true.

It is worth emphasizing that the Hills had no conscious memory of their temporary abduction. They had not reported the UFO sighting to anyone and it is unlikely that they would have done had it not been for Betty's nightmares and Barney's ulcers. Even then they were not looking for fame or publicity, but for an explanation and an end to their problems.

The Hill case remained largely under wraps for many months. The full details did not emerge until the publication of the book *The Interrupted Journey,* written by researcher John Fuller and based on the Hills' account plus some analysis and speculation. The book was an immediate sensation and caught the public imagination.

It was not long before other people came forward to report either abductions or periods of missing time in conjunction with a UFO sighting. Dr Simon, who had hypnotically regressed the Hills, quickly spoke out

> **'It was not long before other people came forward to report either abductions or periods of missing time in conjunction with a UFO sighting.'**

with a word of caution. He made the point that hypnotic regression was not an infallible tool, especially if carried out by a novice to the procedure. It was all too easy for a regressed person to recall a dream or even a movie as if it were something that had really happened to them, and there was always the constant possibility that the hypnotist might unwittingly plant an idea in the patient's mind with a leading question. Indeed, Simon himself was unhappy about a few details of the Hill story, although he did not dismiss the account as a whole. Nevertheless, hypnotic regression has since become a standard tool of UFO research in cases where a missing time episode seems to have occurred during a sighting.

THE SEIZURE OF CHARLES MOODY

One man who was able to recover his memories of a missing time experience over the months following his encounter was Sergeant Charles Moody of the USAF. Moody drove out to a remote desert lay-by at 1 am on the morning of 13 August 1975 to view what the newspapers had billed as a spectacular meteor shower. In the event only a few meteors fell and by 2 am Moody was ready to go home.

It was then that he saw a strange wingless aircraft come diving down to hover about 300 ft (90 m) away. Moody guessed the craft was about 50 ft (15 m) long and 20 ft (6 m) wide with a perfectly smooth, rounded

'The object wobbled slightly, then began to glide towards Moody at walking pace. Moody tried to start his car, but the battery appeared to be dead.'

outline. The object wobbled slightly, then began to glide towards Moody at walking pace. Moody tried to start his car, but the battery appeared to be dead. Then a panel or window opened in the side of the UFO, through which Moody could see human-like figures moving around. Then the panel snapped shut, the object accelerated and flew off at speed.

Charles Moody was able to give a coherent account of his abduction, which included a tour of the UFO and its propulsion unit.

Moody again tried his car, and this time it started perfectly. He drove home to find it was just after 3 am. Over an hour of time was missing from his memory. He was puzzled by the fact that the knuckles on his right hand were scuffed and painful as if he had punched someone, or something, very hard. Over the next few days a rash similar to sunburn broke out over Moody's body while his lower back acquired a dull, throbbing pain. The memory of what happened during the missing time returned slowly to Moody, and by November it was more or less complete.

After the panel opened in the side of the UFO, two of the humanoids had come out. Moody described them as being about 5 ft (1.5 m) tall with rather spindly bodies and limbs, but abnormally large hairless heads. The ears were tiny, the eyes large and the noses small. The skin was of a pale grey colour. He guessed that they weighed around 110 lb (50 kg). Each of the humanoids was dressed in a skin-tight black suit without any visible signs of fastening such as a zip or buttons. Moody said that the figures seemed to glide forward as if hovering rather than walking.

The two figures came up to the car, one reaching out to open the door. Moody decided to fight back. As the creature unlatched the door, Moody kicked it open as violently as he could. The door smashed into the creature, throwing it backwards to sprawl on the ground. Moody then leapt out and ran at the second figure, landing a powerful punch into its face. Then the first alien pointed something at Moody and he blacked out.

He came to lying on a flat, hard table in a large oval room. Beside him stood one of the humanoids, though this one wore a silver suit. Moody tried to sit up, but found himself paralyzed. The being then told Moody that they meant him no harm and asked him if he was still angry and likely to be violent. Moody said that he was not, so the being prodded him with a rod-like instrument. Moody sensed feeling returning to his body, but for some time remained sluggish and clumsy, as if drunk. Moody reported that the alien was talking to him telepathically.

> **'He was puzzled by the fact that the knuckles on his right hand were scuffed and painful as if he had punched someone, or something, very hard.'**

After some conversation about him and his life, Moody asked the alien about the propulsion unit of the UFO, saying that he was interested as he was an aircraft mechanic. The alien led Moody to a lift which took them down to a lower chamber. Unlike the first room, this room was filled with machinery and objects of various kinds. In the centre was a complex arrangement of rods, crystals and balls that rotated and span around each other. There was also a large black box that the alien warned Moody not to touch. He got the impression that it was a weapons system of some kind.

After about twenty minutes in the propulsion room, the alien led Moody back to the upper chamber. There the alien told Moody that the craft they were in was merely a scout ship used to visit Earth's surface. The main spaceship was orbiting the Earth at a height of 6,000 miles (9,600 km). The alien told Moody that he and his comrades were only one of several alien races visiting Earth, though they were all co-operating with each other.

The being then told Moody that the aliens were almost ready to make formal contact with Earth, perhaps within the next three years or so. At first the contact would be limited while the aliens assessed whether Earth's population was ready for more advanced contact. This process might take twenty years or so.

The alien then said it was time to go. He led Moody to a doorway through which the desert and the car could be seen. The alien put its hands on either side of Moody's head, and Moody promptly blacked out. He came to in his car watching the door slam shut and the UFO fly off just as he had originally remembered.

KIDNAP AND EXPERIMENTATION

Rather more intrusive was the experience of David Stephens and his friend, who always preferred to remain anonymous, in Maine on 27 October 1975. The two young men shared a trailer caravan at the town of Norway and worked night shifts. This particular day was a day off, but as they were accustomed to being awake at night both men were up when they heard an explosion at 2.30 am. They went outside to investigate, but saw nothing amiss.

'Suddenly Stephens lost control of the car, which slowed down of its own accord and turned off the road into a field ...'

Stephens suggested driving around to see if they could find anything, the friend agreed and they set off. After a while they saw what they thought was a helicopter flying towards them with navigational lights blazing, but were puzzled by the lack of any engine noise. The object flew to come over the car, then followed the vehicle as Stephens drove back towards Norway. Suddenly Stephens lost control of the car, which slowed down of its own accord and turned off the road into a field overlooking Thompson Lake, where it stopped.

As the two men watched, a round UFO with a dome on top swooped down over the lake, then accelerated towards them as a fog formed over the lake. The fog rolled up to engulf the car, blocking out the surrounding countryside. After a short while the fog lifted and the UFO could be seen accelerating away into the sky.

David Stephens was subjected to a disturbing battery of medical tests by the aliens who abducted him in 1975.

Rather shaken, the two men drove to Stephens' parents' house. They arrived shivering with cold, with puffy eyes and swollen legs and feet. Stephens was in a worse condition than his friend and took several days to recover.

While the friend refused to talk to the press or UFO researchers, Stephens was willing to undergo hypnotic regression. Under hypnosis he recalled that he had been taken from the car by three creatures that emerged from the round UFO after it landed. The friend had been left in the car. The beings were described as being over 4 ft (1.2 m) tall and of basically humanoid shape. Their heads were hairless and large with big eyes, small noses and no ears.

Their arms were thin, ending in hands with three fingers and a thumb that seemed to be webbed. Their skin was of a pale grey or whitish colour. They wore one-piece suits of a black fabric that Stephens likened to brown wrapping paper in texture.

Once inside the UFO, Stephens encountered one creature that was able to communicate with him by telepathy. This being led him to a small room in which there was a flat table with a cushion lying on it. Stephens was asked to lie down on the table, while the creatures took blood samples from him using needles.

The alien able to communicate then told Stephens that they wanted him to undress. He refused, but one

Louise Smith (left), Mona Stafford (centre) and Elaine Thomas (right) who were abducted from their car in Kentucky in 1976.

of the other aliens moved forward and began tugging at his clothes. Stephens lashed out with his fist, striking the creature on the jaw. The alien then backed off, and the talkative one came forward to assure Stephens that they meant him no harm.

After this Stephens undressed himself and lay on the table. A large square machine was wheeled up next to him. A mechanical arm came out carrying what seemed to be a scanning device. This passed up and down the length of Stephens' body several times and the aliens then gave him back his clothes. They seemed to have been inspecting his apparel while the scanning took place, but it was only later that Stephens noticed a button was missing from his jacket.

The aliens then took clippings from his fingernails and hair, putting each sample carefully into a separate jar or phial.

Stephens was then escorted out of the UFO and back into the fog. Next thing he knew he was in the car with his friend watching the UFO depart.

A little-studied but very typical abduction case took place on 6 January 1976. Three ladies in their forties – Louise Smith, Mona Stafford and Elaine Thomas – went out for a meal at a restaurant some forty-five minutes drive north of their homes in Hustonville, Kentucky. They left to drive home at 11.15 pm.

The road passed through isolated rural areas and was quite empty of other vehicles when a UFO appeared. The object was large, perhaps 200 ft

(60 m) across and ringed by a row of red lights that seemed to rotate. The craft's hull seemed to be made of silvery metal, though the dome on top appeared to be white. A cluster of red, blue and yellow lights illuminated the underneath of the object.

The UFO came down to hover over the road in front of the car, then circled round to come behind the vehicle. Smith, who was driving, suddenly realized that the car was accelerating rapidly. She took her foot off the pedals, but this had no effect as the car continued to gather speed. Then the inside of the car was bathed in a bluish-white light of such intensity that it was painful and all three ladies closed their eyes.

When the light blinked off moments later, the women opened their eyes to find that they were coasting sedately into Hustonville. They seemed to have travelled the 8 miles (13 km) to the town in a second or two. Arriving at Smith's house they found the time was 1.25 am, when they should have been home at midnight. Over the following days, all three women suffered eye pain and red weals came up on their skin, only to fade away a few days later.

Other people had seen the UFO that night, though none had had as close an encounter as the three women. This got into the press, and the women added their experiences to the story. This brought the case to the attention of UFO researchers and in July a specialist in hypnotic regression carried out a number of sessions on the women.

'After the bright light entered the car, the vehicle began to shudder and shake violently as if being driven over a rough road at speed.'

Under hypnosis Louise Smith recalled little except that she had been forced to leave the car by somebody, had fluid poured over her face and had experienced great fear. The other two ladies recalled more detail and although their tales do not match exactly, they do not contradict each other.

After the bright light entered the car, the vehicle began to shudder and shake violently as if being driven over a rough road at speed. Then it slowed and seemed to be drawn backwards by some invisible force. The car was then surrounded by humanoids about 4 ft (1.2 m) tall. The creatures had grey skins

The drawing produced by Louise Smith of the humanoid that subjected her to tests that were apparently medical in nature.

and large eyes set on large heads, and were dressed in overalls of a white or pale colour.

The creatures separated the women and led them into different rooms where each was made to lie down on a flat, hard bed or couch. Mona Stafford recalled being scanned by an instrument that looked like a gigantic eye. After this four or five of the creatures moved in to manipulate her arms and legs, squeezing them tightly and causing her pain.

Elaine Thomas recalled having a collar put around her neck. Whenever she tried to speak or call out the collar tightened so much that she began to choke. A number of probes were placed at various points on her body, and then removed.

When the examinations were over, the creatures led the three women out of the UFO and put them back in the car. They were then allowed to drive off.

One odd aspect of the case is that Mrs Smith's pet parakeet would become highly agitated whenever she came close, squawking and flapping around its cage in apparent panic. This reaction lasted for some months after the UFO encounter.

THE DISAPPEARING STREET TRADER

One case that became temporarily famous but has since rather fallen out of favour among researchers was that of Franck Fontaine. On 26 November 1979 three Parisian street traders – Franck Fontaine, Jean-Pierre Prevost and Salomon N'Diaye – got up early to load their van with clothes that they intended to sell at a street market. It was 4 am by the time the van was loaded up.

Fontaine was at the wheel with the engine running when the three men spotted a UFO. The object appeared to be cylindrical, about 50 ft (15 m) across and was approaching slowly. Prevost and N'Diaye ran back into Prevost's flat, where the three men had spent the night. They were looking for Prevost's camera so that they could take a snap of the UFO to sell to the press. While the two men were retrieving the camera, they heard the van engine roar and looked out of the window to see the vehicle accelerating rapidly down the road. Then the engine cut out and the van juddered to a halt. Prevost and N'Diaye raced back out of the building and ran to the car, only to find it empty. Fontaine had gone.

After searching for their friend for an hour or so without result, Prevost and N'Diaye became worried and called the police, who also failed to find any sign of him. At first the police were inclined to ignore the UFO sighting and instead treated Fontaine as a missing person. They began the routine investigations into his finances and family life to see if there were any reasons for him to run off or commit suicide, while the backgrounds of both Prevost and N'Diaye were looked into to see if they had a motive for murder.

Apart from turning up the obvious fact that the three men were street traders who engaged in cash deals for goods that may or may not have been stolen, nothing suspicious was found.

But then news of the disappearance and its UFO link leaked to the Parisian press. They alerted the international media and by 30 November Prevost and N'Diaye were at the centre of a media scrum. They gave interviews, repeating the story time and again. There was still no sign of Fontaine.

The police discovered that two young women, apparently the girlfriends of Prevost and N'Diaye, had stayed in the flat the night before the disappearance. After some initial suspicions it was concluded that they had not come forward because they had not wanted their families to know where they were rather than for any sinister motives.

> 'UFO researchers,
> on the other hand, recognized
> what seemed to be an
> alien abduction and missing time
> episode and moved in.'

On 3 December, seven days after vanishing, Fontaine turned up in a confused state at a friend's house. He said that he thought that he had been asleep, but could not remember how he had left Prevost's flat. He had no idea that an entire week had passed, thinking it was an hour or two later the same morning. Fontaine called the police and was taken in for questioning. The interview proved fruitless as he could remember nothing. Deducing that no crime had been committed, the police dropped the case.

UFO researchers, on the other hand, recognized what seemed to be an alien abduction and missing time episode and moved in. Over the next few weeks, Fontaine began to recall hazy details of what had happened. He remembered being shown into a darkened room by some small figure and made to lie on a hard bed. He remembered seeing a room, the walls of which were lined with machinery and controls. He recalled a glowing sphere that floated in mid-air and spoke to him. He did, however, refuse point blank to be subjected to regressive hypnosis.

Subsequently, Prevost claimed to be a contactee chosen by a group of aliens to be their ambassador to Earth. His tale came with the usual features of a contactee story, complete with a sexy and astonishingly attractive female alien. Most UFO researchers think that he had invented the tale to make money out of his sudden and temporary fame.

Bizarre as the Fontaine case seemed to be at the time, it did in fact have similarities with an event that had taken place in 1975 in Arizona, but which had not by 1979 yet become widely known. On 5 November a gang of woodcutters led by Mike Rogers was working in the forests above the small towns of Heber and Snowflake in the Apache-Sitgreaves National Forest. Their shift ended as dusk closed in. By the time they had packed up their equipment and clambered into the truck to take them home it was 6 pm and almost dark.

Mike Rogers was driving the truck down the track leading towards the main road when the men saw an

The cover of Travis Walton's book about his six-day disappearance, showing the first terrifying moments of his encounter.

object apparently hovering over the trees to one side of the road. As the truck got closer the object could be seen to be disc-shaped and about 20 ft (6 m) wide. It was hovering over a clearing that opened on to the track. Rogers brought the truck to a halt to get a better look.

It was then that one of the workmen, 22-year-old Travis Walton, climbed down and walked forward. He had gone about 50 ft (15 m) when the UFO began to rock gently from side to side and emit a beeping noise that rapidly grew louder to become a booming rumble. The other workmen yelled at Walton to come back. He turned and began to run, but had taken only a couple of steps when a searing shaft of blue-green light erupted from the rim of the saucer. The bolt struck Walton in the back, lifted him clear of the ground and hurled him some 10 ft (3 m) to sprawl motionless on the forest floor.

Terrified and convinced they were about to come under attack, Rogers slammed his foot on the accelerator to send the truck bouncing at top speed down the dirt track. After covering a mile or so, Rogers almost lost control of the vehicle while swerving to take a sharp corner, and slammed on the brakes. The workmen held a hurried debate about what to do. Bravely in the circumstances they decided to head back towards the UFO to retrieve Walton's body – they thought that he had been killed by the blast.

As the truck headed back up the track, they thought that they saw the UFO flying off. When they reached the clearing, about fifteen minutes or so after leaving it, they found that the UFO had indeed gone. So had Walton. The men fanned out into the trees and carried out a hurried search, but they were concerned that the UFO might return and gave up when Walton could not be found. They then drove down to Heber to phone the police and report what had happened.

The police did not believe the story about the UFO. The local sheriff, Marlin Gillespie, was first on the scene. He suspected the woodcutters of drinking or taking drugs. He organized a search of the area around where Walton had gone missing on the assumption that he had become disorientated while drunk and staggered off into the forest. Nothing was found.

When more senior state police became involved they began to suspect foul play of some kind. They grilled the workmen about their relationship with Walton, and looked into Walton's personal life to see if there were any possible motives for suicide or murder. The workmen were subjected to lie detector tests. Of the six men, five produced truthful results when questioned about the UFO and the disappearance of Walton; the sixth gave an inconclusive result.

Then, soon after dawn on 11 November, Walton's brother-in-law got a phone call. 'This is Travis,' came Walton's voice down the line. 'I'm at the Heber gas station and I need help. Come and get me.' The relation was amazed and did not answer at first. 'I'm hurt,' yelled Walton. 'I'm hurt and I need help badly. You come and get me.' This prompted the brother-in-law into speech. After a quick conversation in which he got the impression that Walton was confused, the man drove off to collect him, while alerting police to the development.

Walton was, indeed, confused. He was also weak and suffering from hunger, weight loss and dehydration. After a short spell under medical care, Walton was questioned by police. They quickly concluded that whatever had really happened in the forest, there was no crime to investigate so they released Walton and lost interest.

'Over the following months, Walton was interviewed several times, subjected to lie detector tests and cross-examined at length to try to catch him out.'

As might be expected, UFO researchers were interested. Over the following months, Walton was interviewed several times, subjected to lie detector tests and cross-examined at length to try to catch him out. He passed most tests easily, though he failed the very first lie detector test on a few questions. It later transpired that Walton was still suffering from sleep disorders and nervous twitches when this test was taken, facts which the tester did not know, and that these symptoms may well have affected his reactions.

The tale Walton told matched that of his workmates up until the moment that he turned to run back to the truck. He remembered nothing of the bolt of energy, which had come from behind him, but said he had lost consciousness suddenly. He came to in a clean room, and he initially thought that he was in hospital. He had a metallic taste in his mouth and was struggling to breathe.

The Heber gas station where Travis Walton reappeared after his encounter with the UFO.

Looking around, Walton found that he was lying on a hard table with a band of some sort arching over his chest. The air seemed hot and humid. There were no visible lights but the ceiling and walls seemed to be glowing with a soft white illumination. Apparently noticing that he had regained his senses, three humanoid figures that had been standing nearby now moved towards him.

Walton described the figures as being less than 5 ft (1.5 m) tall and dressed in orange, one-piece suits. He said that they had large, bald heads with domed crowns and high foreheads. Their ears, noses and mouths were tiny. Their eyes, however, were huge, dark brown, and with no whites. They also seemed to have an almost bottomless depth to them. Walton called them 'creepy'.

As the creatures approached, Walton scrambled to his feet (and it seems the band did not prevent him doing this). He grabbed a glass, tube-like object from a nearby table to use as a weapon and prepared to defend himself. The beings stopped, regarded Walton for a few seconds and then retreated out of the room. Walton followed and found himself in a curving corridor. He found a door and went through it into a room that was empty except for a large chair with buttons and dials along the armrests.

As Walton approached the chair, the lights in the room dimmed and the walls became see-through. He approached and retreated several times, and each time the lights dimmed. Finally he sat in the chair, at which point the lights went out completely and the ceiling became entirely transparent. Above him Walton could see stars.

Idly, he began to fiddle with the dials and buttons on the chair arm. The stars above him began to rotate as if he were in a planetarium. Then the lights abruptly came back on and Walton saw a figure coming in through the door. The figure was about the height of a human, and was roughly human in form though it appeared to be heavily muscled. Walton

'The humanoids all turned to look at Walton. They were smiling and giving off an aura of friendliness. Then they pounced on Walton, forced a mask over his face ...'

assumed the figure was male and got the feeling that he was friendly. The most arresting features of the new arrival were his eyes, which were a bright golden-hazel colour.

The man led Walton out, down a corridor and through a cubicle-like room. This gave access to a vast room rather like an aircraft hangar. Looking behind him, Walton saw that he had emerged from the UFO he had seen in the woods. Three or four other similar craft were parked in the hangar. The alien led Walton past these and into a room in which stood three other similar figures.

The humanoids all turned to look at Walton. They were smiling and giving off an aura of friendliness. Then they pounced on Walton, forced a mask over his face and pushed him forcibly down on to a table. Walton lost consciousness a second time.

The next thing he remembered was coming to while lying face up beside the highway near to Heber. A light in the sky, which may have been the UFO, was flying off. Picking himself up, Walton slowly realized where he was – about 10 miles (16 km) from where he had encountered the UFO. Blundering into town, he found a payphone from where he called his brother-in-law.

Travis Walton (centre) photographed a few months after his encounter. He suffered no long term ill effects from his experience.

Opinion among UFO researchers to Walton's adventure was mixed. It took some time for the details to come out. When Walton wrote a book on the subject that contained much extraneous material and speculation, some suspected that he had invented the whole tale to earn money. Others thought the book to be an entirely respectable attempt to explain what had happened and to make some cash from an event that had stopped Walton from working and disrupted his personal life. A movie based on the book was made in 1993, but Walton disowned it as it contained entirely fictional sequences inside the UFO very different from what he said had happened.

Whitley Strieber, one of the first people to report having been abducted by aliens from inside his own house.

BEDROOM ABDUCTIONS

A whole new form of alien abduction was heralded by the experiences of Whitley Strieber in 1985. On the night of 4 October, Strieber, his wife and son were staying at the family's log cabin in upstate New York. At some point in the night Strieber woke up to see the room suffused in a blue glow. He was puzzled, but fell asleep again.

A while later he and his wife were awoken by a loud bang. This time the room was bathed in a brighter light while a fog surrounded the house. Thinking the house was on fire, Strieber told his wife to wake up their son while he went to tackle the blaze. A few seconds later the light went out and the fog dispersed. There was nothing wrong with the house at all.

The son was found to be downstairs. He said that he had heard a bang, but that a 'small doctor' had told him not to worry as the noise had been caused by his father hitting a fly with a shoe. When told he had been dreaming, the boy replied, 'It was a strange dream. It was just like for real.' Over the following weeks, Strieber began to suffer bad dreams featuring a gigantic crystal pillar.

The family returned to the cabin for Christmas. On the night of 26 December, Strieber was again woken by a noise though this time his wife slept on. He looked around and saw a small humanoid figure in a corner of the room. The figure rushed at him. Strieber blacked out. He came to lying on his back in the forest, and then fainted again. The next thing he remembered was being in a circular room where he heard the sounds of people moving around. Then a sharp needle was pushed into his brain causing extreme agony, while a second probe was pushed up his bottom. Then he fainted again and woke up back in his bed.

After this, Strieber contacted UFO researchers and voluntarily underwent regressive hypnosis. This filled in the gaps left in his conscious memory of the events of 26 December. Under hypnosis he was able to give a clearer description of the humanoid that had appeared in his bedroom. He said the figure had looked like a goblin with an ugly face, pointed ears and large eyes. It had worn a cape-like garment.

This alien had paralyzed Strieber with a rod-like instrument. Then other goblin-like figures had appeared and dragged Strieber outside. They had taken off his pyjamas and strapped him to a chair. With a sudden whooshing sound, the chair had been thrown hundreds of feet into the air to enter a UFO hovering above.

Inside the UFO was a female alien in a beige, one-piece suit. She addressed him as 'the chosen one' and tried to induce him to have sex with her. Strieber refused despite her sensual advances, after which she became angry. What happened next could not be remembered even under hypnosis. The next thing Strieber could recall was waking up naked in the lounge of the cabin. He put on his pyjamas and returned to bed to fall asleep and forget most of what had happened.

VICTIM OR STORYTELLER?

The fact that Strieber was a writer of moderately successful horror novels caused some UFO researchers to treat his claims with caution. They thought that the tale of an abduction from the safety of a bedroom was more like a horror movie than a classic UFO abduction event.

Shortly afterwards, Strieber began to suffer nosebleeds and received anonymous phone calls with threatening messages akin to those given by Men in Black. Strieber decided to give up his career as a horror writer and instead became a UFO researcher. He has produced a number of books since, keeping

After his abduction, Strieber began receiving anonymous and deeply unpleasant telephone calls.

an open mind on what the explanation might be. He does not espouse the theory that UFOs are alien spacecraft, but prefers to examine the evidence without such a preconceived idea.

> **'Some witnesses claim to have been abducted repeatedly over a period of years. They say that they know that an abduction has occurred overnight when they wake up in unusual circumstances.'**

Strieber's experiences were the first to be publicized in a succession of what would become known as 'bedroom abductions'. These events have in common the fact that the witness does not recall any type of UFO encounter or a lost time episode to prompt a hypnotic regression. Instead the suspicion that something may be wrong is usually triggered by sleep disorders, nightmares and fragmentary memories. A few witnesses can recall the events by themselves, while others need regressive hypnotic treatment to access their memory.

Some witnesses claim to have been abducted repeatedly over a period of years. They say that they know that an abduction has occurred overnight when they wake up in unusual circumstances. Either their pyjamas are on inside out, or their nightdress back to front, or they wake up on the downstairs sofa instead of in bed. These are all, the witnesses say, an indication that an abduction has taken place.

Hypnotic regression usually reveals a memory of an encounter with aliens and their medical procedures.

Generally the abduction begins in the bedroom, though sometimes in another room, when the witness is roused by a loud bang or by the sounds of people moving about the house. On waking, the witness sees an alien either in the room or entering – usually by the door but sometimes by drifting through the walls. The witness is then paralyzed and floated off to enter a UFO, or sometimes to materialize directly in an examination chamber.

The encounter then progresses along similar lines to a more normal abduction. The witness is subjected to a variety of medical examinations and procedures. Sometimes the witness is allowed to visit different parts of the UFO. In all cases, the witnesses are then transported back to their bedroom before having their memories wiped.

In contrast to the more usual abductions, bedroom abductions always happen to individual persons. If another person is sleeping in the room at the time, they are not involved and have no recollection of anything having happened at all.

THE MANHATTAN TRANSFER CASE

The lack of any form of corroborative evidence led some to suggest that the events were nothing more than dreams. Then what became known as the Manhattan Transfer case came to light in 1996. The main witness was a New York housewife who at first

Linda Napolitano, the woman at the centre of the highly controversial and complex 'Manhattan Transfer' case.

used the name Linda Cortile, but who later revealed that her real name was Linda Napolitano.

The case began on 30 November 1989 when Napolitano contacted noted UFO researcher Bud Hopkins to report that the previous night she had suddenly awoken at 3.15 am to see what looked like an alien in her bedroom. She had thrown her pillow at the figure, then blacked out and come to some time later falling from a height on to her bed.

Recognizing a typical bedroom abduction case, Hopkins went to investigate and persuaded Napolitano to undergo hypnotic regression. Under hypnosis she revealed a fairly typical experience. There had, in fact, been three aliens in her bedroom. They were described as being short, grey-skinned and with large heads. The aliens had paralyzed Napolitano, then a beam of intense blue light had come shafting into the room through the window. Napolitano floated up along this beam of light and

out of the window, which was closed at the time, to drift over the street and up into a UFO that was hovering overhead.

Inside the UFO, Napolitano was subjected to medical examinations. She was then transported back along the beam of light to float a couple of feet above the bed. When the light was switched off she fell heavily on to the mattress, which was when her conscious memory took over.

Hopkins carried out further investigations, but then filed the case away with his others. In February 1991, however, the Napolitano case suddenly became of interest again when Hopkins got a letter from two men claiming to be New York police officers who had seen a UFO beam a woman up on a blue shaft of light. By checking dates, times and locations Hopkins realized that the policemen were referring to the Napolitano case. The letter said the UFO had then flown off to dive into the East River and had disappeared. They had waited for forty-five minutes, but then duty called and they had to move on. They asked Hopkins if the woman was safe, and signed themselves Richard and Dan.

A short time later two men claiming to be Richard and Dan called on Napolitano. They said they wanted to remain anonymous as they were really secret service agents. In a later letter to Hopkins, Richard and Dan said that they had been driving 'a high-ranking international political figure' through New York when their car suddenly stopped working. All

At the start of her abduction, Linda Napolitano was transported up a beam of light along with the aliens who were kidnapping her.

three men had then witnessed the UFO coming down and the abduction of Napolitano taking place.

Later speculation named UN chief Javier Perez de Cuellar as the third man, though this is conjectural. When de Cuellar was contacted on the subject he denied even being near the place at the time, saying that he had been at home in bed all night long.

Hopkins hypothesized that the aliens had stopped the car carrying the third man and the secret agents and had then abducted a person in a way that the three men could not possibly miss. The purpose was, Hopkins said, to show a respected world leader that abductions were true.

Hopkins then put a lot more effort into the case. He found several witnesses who lived near Napolitano's apartment block who recalled seeing a UFO on the night in question. One saw the shaft of blue light and thought she saw objects floating along it.

When Hopkins revealed his evidence in a book entitled *Witnessed* in 1996 it seemed to offer evidence that bedroom abductions were every bit as real, perhaps more so, than the more usual situations. But then the case began to turn peculiar. In April 1991, Dan and Richard returned and bundled Napolitano into a car. They drove her around while asking her a series of bizarre questions, such as asking how many toes she had. The car they were driving was being followed by another which carried diplomatic plates.

Then Hopkins received a letter from Dan that claimed that he, Richard and the third man had since recovered further memories of the night and now realized that they too had been abducted. They had been flown to a beach where they had seen Napolitano building sandcastles with the aliens. She had then picked up a dead fish and waved it at the third man accusing him of leading humanity's pollution of the world's oceans. When Dan asked what right she had to make accusations, one of the aliens had interrupted to say that Napolitano was 'our lady of the sands'.

Bud Hopkins, who investigated the Manhattan Transfer case.

Napolitano then received another weird visit from Dan and Richard. Soon after this she got a long, rambling letter from Dan saying that he had been confined to a mental hospital. Richard subsequently wrote to Hopkins several times claiming repeated abductions of increasingly bizarre aspect. Although some researchers continued to believe that the case offered firm evidence of the reality of bedroom abductions, others felt that it had been undermined by the later revelations.

Among those who came to disbelieve the evidence, opinion was divided as to whether Napolitano and

Hopkins had been the victims of a prank, or whether the assorted witnesses, and in particular Dan and Richard, had been agents acting on behalf of security services intent on discrediting the whole UFO scenario.

IS HYPNOSIS RELIABLE?

In considering the phenomenon of alien abductions, it is important to bear in mind the limitations of hypnotic regression. As Dr Simon stated in relation to the Hill case, it is an imprecise science. It is all too easy for the interviewer to inadvertently plant ideas into the mind of the witness, and for these to come back as 'memories', and it is also possible for the person being regressed to recall a movie or dream as if it happened to them as a real event.

Rather less well known is the fact that the regression very rarely follows a strictly chronological path through the event being remembered. Under hypnosis, the witness does not say, 'I saw a UFO, it looked like this. Then an alien appeared, it looked like this. Then I went on board. The alien produced a scanner and began medical tests.' What is much more typical is that the witness recalls disjointed scenes and events as the recovered memories force themselves out through the hypnotic trance. The individual scenes may be repeated, enlarged upon and repeated again if they are important to the witness, or passed over hurriedly if not. What makes one event important to an abductee and another less important is unknown.

> **'Rather less well known is the fact that the regression very rarely follows a strictly chronological path through the event being remembered.'**

Annoyingly for the researcher the witnesses usually find the interaction with the alien more important than more mundane but relevant facts such as how the UFO worked or what it looked like. Typically the eyes of the aliens are of paramount interest to the witnesses, who talk about them at great length.

A transcript of a hypnotic regression session follows, relating to a witness who was abducted in 1974. The interviewer is trying to elicit information about how the witness conversed with the alien.

Interviewer: How does he say this? Does he speak it?

Witness: No. His brain. Maybe that's what the glow is around his head. That's how they communicate.

Interviewer: With the glow around them?

Witness: Yes.

Interviewer: I don't understand. How does he communicate with that?

Witness: Well, they don't talk [pause] and yet they know what I'm thinking.

Interviewer: What are you thinking?

Witness: The fact that I want to know them, or what's going on.

Interviewer: Does he say anything to you?

Witness: He sort of thinks a lot of things at me.

Putting together a coherent account of what happened during an abduction can be a slow and difficult business, and is not always possible. Most abductees do not recall a chronological account of their abduction, even under hypnotic regression. The cases described above are unusual in that the witness has been able to tell a story that is both clear and internally consistent. Most abductees give an account that is disjointed, often obscure and usually confused.

Nevertheless, when taken as a whole the vast mass of accounts do have a lot of features in common. These include the process through which the abduction takes place and the different stages that occur as well as similarities between descriptions of the aliens and how they behave.

THE FIVE STAGES OF AN ALIEN ABDUCTION

There are five generally recognized stages of an abduction. The first occurs in the normal surroundings of the witness. This very often begins with a UFO being seen to land and humanoid entities to emerge, but in the case of bedroom abductions a figure appears in the home of the witness without a UFO being seen. The stage continues with the witness being paralyzed, rendered unconscious or otherwise made helpless. The witness is then carried or floated into a waiting UFO, or sometimes transported directly into an examination chamber.

The second phase begins in a room of some kind, most often presumed to be inside the UFO. The witness is usually undressed before being subjected to medical procedures. This often involves intrusive and sometimes very painful procedures such as needles and probes being pushed into the witness. The most popular parts of the body for these probes seem to be the nose and nasal cavity and the reproductive organs. The nose is often scraped to gain tissue samples, or a long needle is inserted in order to either place or remove a small metallic implant. The attention given to the reproductive organs seems designed to secure samples of eggs or sperm.

There then follows an examination. This may involve the aliens moving the human's limbs about, or sophisticated devices of some kind may be used to scan the witness. These sometimes take the form of a gigantic lens or eye. Sometimes the witness is allowed to view the results of this examination on a monitor, but the data rarely makes any sense and is never explained. Sometimes the examination comes before the medical procedures.

The fourth phase is often bizarre and frequently unique to the individual witness. It begins with the witness being led out of the examination chamber and taken on a tour of the UFO. When taken into another room the witness may be forcibly immersed in a large tank of liquid, subjected to agonizingly painful tortures that seem designed to test pain

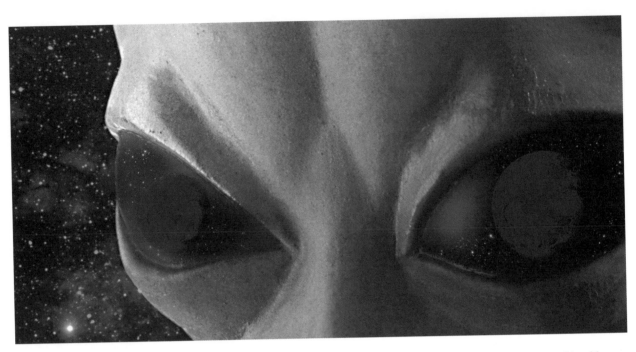

Most victims of alien abduction report that the aliens involved were of the type now called 'greys', diminutive humanoids with grey skin and huge almond-shaped eyes.

thresholds, or else given medicines to cure some disease that the alien alleges the witness has contracted. Some witnesses report being encouraged to have sex either with aliens or with a fellow human captive. Some female abductees say that they are given a sickly baby to hold and cuddle.

The fifth and final phase comes when the witness is returned to the normal world. Usually the witness has no conscious memory of what has happened. The memory may return later, but more often is revealed in dreams or by way of hypnotic regression. Some witnesses have experiences towards the end of the abduction that hint that the aliens may be deliberately wiping their memories, but this is by no means clear.

'GREYS'

The descriptions of the aliens encountered during abductions almost always relate to a type of creature that is known in UFO circles as the 'grey'. These greys are described as being around 4 ft (1.2 m) tall with skins of a pale grey or off-white colour. They have abnormally large heads which are totally hairless and feature tiny noses, ears and mouths. Their eyes by contrast are huge, usually being said to be totally black and oval in shape. Their torsos and limbs are described as being spindly, though the beings can exhibit great strength when they want to do so. Their arms end in hands with elongated fingers, sometimes only three being present. Some witnesses report that the eyes seem to be a communication device, with

telepathic messages being transferred through the alien's eyes into those of the witness. If the alien is not looking into the witness's eyes, telepathic communication cannot take place.

There are variations within the greys. The vast majority of them are short. These beings appear to be quite indifferent to their human victims, behaving as a human scientist might do towards an ant. They display no emotions and exhibit no concern for the pain that their human victim experiences.

A few witnesses report that the greys seem to be working for, or are under the instructions of, a different type of being. These seem to be more human in appearance and have a skin colour often described as tan or ochre. Unlike the greys these aliens seem to be male or female rather than androgynous. They show some concern for the human witness, often behaving in a friendly manner or seeking to calm the abductee. It is these taller aliens who are said to engage in conversations with witnesses, as opposed to the sharp instructions issued by the greys.

Opinions are divided on what the alien abduction experiences mean. Sceptics argue that many people are simply inventing their experiences either in the hope of cashing in, for mischievous motives of trickery or for some other reason known only to them. It has also been pointed out that the vast majority of alleged abductions have taken place only since movies and books publicized the claims of the Hills,

'... reports of implants being put into abductees' heads and other parts of their bodies ... These have shown up on X-rays as tiny metallic objects buried deep in a victim's brain.

Antonio Villas Boas and a handful of other early witnesses. Perhaps the witnesses are reporting very vivid dreams based on those accounts.

Others point out that the vast majority of witnesses make similar statements and seem to have undergone similar experiences. This would seem to indicate that they are reporting real events and real procedures. But even among those who believe that alien abductions are real there are disputes about what is going on.

Some researchers have focused on the reports of implants being put into abductees' heads and other parts of their bodies. These are usually described as being minute. A few have shown up on X-rays as tiny metallic objects buried deep in a victim's brain. There is no known surgical procedure for extracting these, so they remain unstudied. One implant that was removed from the penis of an abducted man turned out to be a 15 mm-long strip of very thin material. When analyzed the strip proved to be composed of carbon, silicon, oxygen and various trace elements. It was not a naturally occurring compound, but beyond that analysis revealed nothing. Another implant

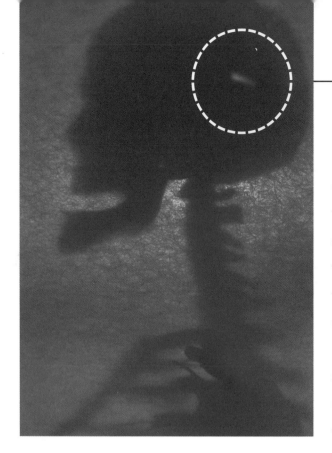

An X-ray that shows what purports to be an alien implant.

turned out to be metal encased in a covering of a material that seemed to be a blend of keratin and hemosiderin, both naturally occurring products of mammalian bodies.

It has been suggested that the implants are used by the aliens to monitor the human body into which they are put. Others think that they may be the way in which aliens are able to snatch the same person several times while most people never suffer an abduction. Perhaps the aliens are able to detect the implant, and home in on it to conduct an abduction. In other words they may perform a function similar to that of the rings used by scientists studying birds.

Other researchers have been more impressed by the nature of the medical procedures and examinations that are reported. Many of these focus on the reproductive organs. There are also numerous reports of attempted or actual sexual acts with aliens or between human captives. To this should be added the reports by female abductees that they are given sickly infants to hold and cuddle for a while during their experience. A very few abductees are told that the infants are human-alien hybrids that are ailing due to a lack of human mother love.

It has been speculated that the main purpose of abductions is to produce human-alien hybrids. Some researchers think that the repeated abductions of women of child-bearing age points to one aspect of this breeding programme. It is speculated that the woman is abducted the first time to have a hybrid egg implanted into her womb, then a second time a few weeks later to have the embryo removed to continue its development by some other means.

Why this should be an objective of the aliens is unclear. Some think that they may be suffering genetic problems and need an injection of human genes to rectify this. Others think that the hybrid race is being produced to act as a workforce, perhaps on a planet where the aliens cannot themselves live. Or it may be that the aliens realize that humanity is doomed and seek to preserve something of the human genetic inheritance. This scenario harks back to the doom-laden warnings so often passed on to contactees and to a few abductees.

Since the first abduction cases became widely known among UFO researchers, abductions have come to dominate some discussions of the UFO

The fictional spaceship USS *Enterprise* from the television series *Star Trek – the Next Generation*, which featured a storyline about alien abductions.

phenomenon. The concept was even made the centrepiece of an episode of the fictional and highly popular TV series, *Star Trek – The Next Generation.*

In some ways it has come to overshadow the actual UFOs themselves. Many researchers have become convinced that the answer to the UFO conundrum is to be found through the study of abductions. Others consider these kidnappings to be something of a blind alley that will prove fruitless to explore.

Above all there have been increasing concerns about the use of hypnotic regression as a means of recovering useable evidence. The use of the technique by untrained researchers is controversial. Some medical doctors have voiced concerns that such sessions might lead to psychological problems. Several UFO research groups have dropped the practice altogether, while others insist that it be carried out only by a trained practitioner.

That said, the abduction experience does include a large number of cases that appear to be independent of each other and that offer valuable details about what seem to be aliens visiting Earth. The problem is how this evidence fits in with data collected elsewhere and by other means.

The people best placed to make such deductions and evaluations are those who are studying UFOs as a serious discipline. Over the years there have been, and still are, many such individuals.

'... the woman is abducted the first time to have a hybrid egg implanted into her womb, then a second time a few weeks later to have the embryo removed to continue its development by some other means.'

CHAPTER 6

THE SEARCH FOR TRUTH

Ever since the first UFO was spotted back in 1947 there have been people investigating the phenomenon. While these investigations have varied greatly both in their intent and the ability of the investigators, they have tended to fall into two main categories: official investigations by the military or government agencies and those undertaken by private individuals.

Over the years there has been a fair degree of misunderstanding and mutual suspicion between the two camps of investigators. In large part this was due to the fact that the earliest official probes in the later 1940s and early 1950s were conducted in secret, with no announcements about the results being made public.

At the time this all seemed reasonable enough. Nobody knew what UFOs were, where they came from or what the purpose of their controllers might be. They were viewed as being a possible and very potent threat to the security of the nation whose government was undertaking the inquiries. Most private researchers were as baffled as to the nature of the UFOs as were the officials. They were inclined to trust the official investigators to seek diligently after the truth.

As time passed, however, those members of the public who had an interest in UFOs began to get frustrated by the official studies. Although the government sources claimed repeatedly that there was nothing to investigate, they refused to release their files. This led to the suspicion that the governments of the world were hiding something, that they were covering up the truth.

The assorted government agencies that have dealt with UFO investigations have never been able to shake off this reputation for obfuscation and deceit. The fact that they are known to have hidden secrets in the past has led to the not unnatural assumption that they are still hiding facts about UFOs and aliens.

'The assorted government agencies that have dealt with UFO investigations have never been able to shake off this reputation for obfuscation and deceit.'

Private investigators, on the other hand, have tended to be far more open about their findings. In fact, this has sometimes led to problems when they have made announcements of 'revelations' that have turned out to be either mistaken or based on fraud. As a consequence some private investigators have gained a reputation for being unreliable, and in the public mind this tag has tended to spread to even the most diligent of researchers.

Another long-running problem besetting the private investigators has been a lack of money. Neither universities nor business concerns have tended to fund research into UFOs. Instead the researchers have depended on private donations and funds raised by book sales, media deals and other merchandising. Inevitably this has led some to suspect that the researchers may be inclined to exaggerate their findings in the hope of maximizing book sales or advances from the media. The stories produced by a handful of hoaxers and fraudsters have only made this situation worse.

It is very often in the interplay between the various individuals and organizations investigating UFOs that the theories and ideas to explain the phenomenon have developed. No single body has had a greater influence, both intended and unintended, on the UFO story than has the United States Air Force (USAF).

> ## 'No single body has had a greater influence, both intended and unintended, on the UFO story than has the United States Air Force (USAF).'

PROJECT SIGN

When Kenneth Arnold reported his flying saucer sighting in the summer of 1947 he went to see the FBI because he was concerned that what he saw might be some type of secret weapon being tested by a foreign power, specifically the USSR. It was this worry that prompted the USAF to set up Project Sign to investigate the flying saucers.

Sign was prompted into being because of a letter sent by Lieutenant General Nathan F. Twining, commander of the Air Materiel Command to the head of the USAF, Brigadier General George Shulgen. The letter summarized the short initial investigation undertaken by Twining on the instructions of Shulgen.

Twining's letter briefly reviewed the sightings known to that date and gave an estimate of the size and capabilities of the aircraft being seen – the assumption at this point was still that flying saucers were aircraft. It then stated that: 'The phenomenon reported is something real, not visionary or fictitious.' Although it accepted that 'some of the incidents may be caused by natural phenomena, such as meteors' it concluded that 'there are objects approximating the shape of a disc and of such appreciable size as to appear to be as large as man-made aircraft', while cautioning that a lack of any hard evidence – such as a retrieved crash – meant that there was nothing to 'undeniably prove the existence of these objects'.

The letter put forward two possible origins for the saucers. Firstly: 'The possibility that these objects are of domestic origin – the product of some high security project not known to this Command.' In other words, a private business or government agency within the USA had secretly produced aircraft of the size, shape and abilities of the flying saucers. Secondly: 'The possibility that some foreign nation has a form of propulsion, possibly nuclear, which is outside of our domestic knowledge.'

The report went on to make a number of recommendations. One was for the USAF high

General Nathan Twining initiated the first official US military investigation into UFOs in 1947. Twining was convinced that something real was going on.

command to make inquiries that would rule out an origin for the saucers within the USA. If that could be dismissed, then the letter suggested that the USAF should 'issue a directive assigning a priority, security classification and code name for a detailed study of this matter.'

The USAF did as Twining suggested. Having ruled out a US origin for the saucers, it set up Project Sign on 30 December 1947. The investigatory team was stationed at Wright-Patterson Air Force Base in Ohio and was given authority to use members of the Air Technical Intelligence Centre (ATIC), which was also based at Wright-Patterson.

It should be noted that the Twining letter and the resulting Project Sign dated from after the alleged

UFO crash at Roswell. Those who do not believe that the reports from Roswell amount to proof of a crash use the Twining letter to demonstrate that nothing happened in New Mexico. After all, the Twining letter specifically states that no UFO had been known to crash and been retrieved.

Those investigators who are inclined to believe that a UFO did crash at Roswell see the Twining letter and subsequent events as being proof that the USAF cover-up had begun early. They point out that the Twining letter was classified as 'secret', which is actually a fairly low security classification. Even if Twining had known about a UFO crash at Roswell, he would not have referred to it in a document with only a 'secret' classification.

Under this scenario, the USAF was starting an entirely bogus investigation with the intention of later releasing the documents to 'prove' that UFOs did not exist. Meanwhile the real investigation was taking place amid the highest possible levels of secrecy.

Whatever view one may take as to the actions of the USAF, it is known that late in 1948 Project Sign produced a document that was classified as 'top secret' and entitled 'Estimate of the Situation'. This report dealt only with a fairly limited number of UFO reports. They were those that had been made by entirely trustworthy individuals, including USAF pilots and government scientists and which featured sightings that could not be dismissed as natural phenomena of any kind.

The Estimate of the Situation concluded that the UFOs were real, solid objects that were capable of speeds and manoeuvres beyond those of any aircraft known to the USAF. They also concluded that because some UFOs had taken evasive manoeuvres when approached by aircraft, they must be under intelligent control – either by a crew inside the UFO or via some form of remote control. From these the report deduced that the UFOs were almost certainly not produced by either a secret private venture or by a foreign government. It suggested that an alien origin was the most likely.

When this report reached the desk of General Hoyt Vandenberg, head of the USAF, it caused a sensation. Vandenberg read it carefully, then announced that the conclusions were not supported by the evidence. He ordered the destruction of all copies of the report. Those men who had favoured the alien origin of UFOs were dismissed from Project Sign.

THE TRUTH IS OUT THERE – OR IS IT?

In February 1949 Sign was closed down and Project Grudge initiated to take its place. Vandenberg gave Grudge the specific instruction that it was to make every effort to find a conventional explanation for each and every UFO sighting made to it. On no account was even the suggestion of an alien origin to be given. If no conventional explanation could be found, a case was to be designated as 'unexplained'.

True to its instructions, Grudge set out to discredit

J. Allen Hynek was an astronomer who was at first sceptical about UFOs, but later became convinced that they were real.

the case for the reality of UFOs. Even if the evidence did not really support a conclusion that a sighting had been of a meteor, weather balloon or aircraft, that would be the explanation put forward. Notoriously, Grudge personnel undertook research into the private lives of witnesses and used any evidence of heavy drinking or emotional problems as evidence of an unbalanced mental state so that the report could be written off. In general, the details of any Grudge investigation were kept secret and only the conclusions issued to the press and public.

By the end of 1949 the USAF high command concluded that Grudge had completed its task. Reports of flying saucers were no longer being taken seriously by the national press. Grudge was closed down. Years later in 1978, what was alleged to be the true, internal view of the Grudge team was released by a former officer named Captain William English. This 'Grudge Report 13' stated that not only were UFOs real, but that they were piloted by aliens. It is generally dismissed as a hoax but, as we shall see, the truth may not be that simple.

After Grudge was terminated, all UFO reports made to the authorities in the USA were channelled to ATIC. By 1952 the staff at ATIC were making objections to this system. Reports were coming in from all over the country, from military as well as civilian sources. These reports were not investigated, being merely filed away and a neutral letter sent assuring the witness that UFOs did not exist. Witnesses were not content to be dismissed in this way, and the growing bands of private investigators were making their discontent felt as well. The press were starting to take notice.

FURTHER INVESTIGATIONS

In March 1952 the USAF established Project Blue Book to handle the developing need for some improved form of public relations to deal with witnesses and the media. This organization had Captain Edward Ruppelt as its first chief. It was staffed by a small number of junior officers, several of whom worked on it only part-time. Ruppelt had a budget that allowed him to call in outside consultants with expertise in a relevant area.

One of these was the astronomer J. Allen Hynek. His task was to see if any of the reports might be sightings of natural objects such as meteors seen under unusual conditions. Hynek would later come to play a role as a private investigator.

Blue Book, meanwhile, continued primarily as a public relations operation. The personnel investigated only those cases where the media was taking an interest. All investigations had as their primary objective the finding of a conventional explanation for the sighting. Once the media lost interest, so did Blue Book. As with Grudge, the details of any

'Only in extreme cases did Blue Book designate a sighting as "unexplained". Most sightings were never investigated at all, but were simply filed.'

investigations were kept secret and only the conclusions released to the public. These conclusions generally stated that the witness had been mistaken in what they reported and had, in fact, seen a meteor, a weather balloon, a military jet or some such rational explanation. Only in extreme cases did Blue Book designate a sighting as 'unexplained'. Most sightings were never investigated at all, but were simply filed.

In recent years the secret Blue Book files have been made public, and in 2008 went on to the internet. Researchers had long hoped that the secret files contained a wealth of information and, perhaps, evidence that the USAF had something to hide. In fact they revealed only that the Blue Book officers had

'... the CIA had carefully screened the panel before it even met by inviting only those scientists known to oppose an alien explanation for UFOs.'

been short of funds, short of time and short of resources. There were reports in large numbers and some of them made very interesting reading. But the reports were all many decades old by the time they became public and the original witnesses were unavailable for further questioning. Above all there was no 'smoking gun' to prove any government cover-up conspiracy.

The official reason for this was that by the time that Blue Book had been set up, the USAF had lost any real interest in the UFO phenomenon. Such reports as had been studied in depth during the period 1947 to 1952 had revealed that whatever UFOs were, they were not a threat to the security of the USA. Since the prime task of the USAF was to protect the air space over the USA from foreign attack, the antics of UFOs were of no interest to it. This, at least, was the official explanation given some years later.

That this was not entirely true was shown when CIA documents were released under freedom of information legislation in the 1990s. These documents related to the Robertson Panel, a body set up by the CIA in January 1953 to study the UFO phenomenon.

Officially, the Robertson Panel was founded to investigate UFO reports in an impartial manner. It was composed of a group of top level scientists led by a physicist, Dr H. Robertson of the California Institute of Technology. They were to review investigations into seventy-five of the best-documented UFO reports that defied explanation in conventional terms. In fact, as is now known, the CIA had carefully screened the panel before it even met by inviting only those scientists known to oppose an alien explanation for UFOs.

After lengthy deliberations, the panel produced the sort of report the CIA wanted. It stated that there was no evidence to show that UFOs were alien craft, or indeed that they were solid objects at all. Any threat from UFOs was dismissed out of hand and the idea that they were worthy of official investigation by the US government ridiculed.

What had been bothering the CIA was revealed in the 1990s. It was responsible for collecting and collating information on potential enemy states and their military capabilities. Ultimately, the CIA had to provide the US military both with an accurate assessment of any enemy military force and with clear guidelines on who to recognize as an attacker when it came. In the age before intercontinental missiles, this meant giving the USAF a description of any and all Soviet aircraft capable of carrying atomic bombs into US air space.

The reports of UFOs were causing the CIA problems on two fronts. Firstly, they induced confusion as to what the Soviets and other air forces were capable of producing. Secondly, they served to mask sightings of real intruding aircraft. There was a genuine worry that a Soviet air strike might be preceded by a number of communist agents in the USA and in the territories of her allies making a large number of false UFO reports. This might cause the USAF to dismiss reports of incoming aircraft as being false UFO sightings when they were in fact approaching Soviet bombers.

> **'There is evidence to suggest that the CIA put agents into some UFO investigatory groups both to check for communist agents and to spread disinformation.'**

By dismissing UFOs as unworthy of comment, it was hoped that UFO reports from the public would be discouraged and quashed. That would leave the USAF with only real intruders to investigate. There is evidence to suggest that the CIA put agents into some UFO investigatory groups both to check for communist agents and to spread disinformation. It seems that the FBI has also taken part in such activities.

After the publication of the Robertson Panel's report both the CIA and FBI consistently denied having any interest in either UFOs or the civilians who investigate them. However, freedom of information requests in the 1990s and 2000s showed that both organizations continued to take an interest. The combination of official denial and subsequent revelation has persuaded many researchers that the CIA and FBI are more heavily involved than has become apparent.

CONCLUSION AND OMISSION

Meanwhile, Project Blue Book continued to operate after the Robertson Panel report. In 1956 Captain Edward Ruppelt, by then retired, produced a book called *The Report on Unidentified Flying Objects.* The book was largely a review of material already in the public domain, but caused great excitement as Ruppelt was known to be privy to the Blue Book files. His conclusion that UFOs were almost certainly alien spacecraft caused a sensation. When the book was reprinted the conclusion was omitted. Many suspected that Ruppelt had been persuaded to change his mind by the USAF.

In 1968 a new government-sponsored assignment, the Condon Committee, was formed to look at UFOs. This body was paid for by the USAF itself and chaired by Edward Condon. As with the Robertson Panel, those taking part were screened beforehand to ensure that they did not believe that UFOs were alien spacecraft. As with the earlier body, the Condon Committee produced the report that its paymasters wanted. Despite inspecting a wide range of high quality reports – including a description of an early abduction – Edward Condon's declaration dismissed the entire UFO phenomenon.

From 1963 Lt Col Hector Quintanilla headed the USAF investigation Project Blue Book which investigated all reports of UFOs made to the US military. He concluded that there was no evidence that UFOs were alien spacecraft.

As soon as the Condon Committee announced its findings, the USAF reached the conclusion that 'the continuation of the Project Blue Book cannot be justified either on the grounds of national security or in the interest of science.' Blue Book was disbanded.

Before it closed down, Blue Book issued a series of thirteen special reports that summarized its activities since it had been founded and reviewed the more interesting cases. These concluded that: 'No UFO reported, investigated and evaluated by the Air Force has ever given any indication of a threat to our national security,' and that 'there has been no evidence indicating that sightings categorized as "unidentified" are extraterrestrial vehicles.'

AN END TO INVESTIGATIONS?

With the publication of these reports, all official interest on the part of the US military and government on the subject of UFOs came to an end. At least, it came to an end officially. Documents have emerged since by way of leaks and freedom of information requests that show the military is still interested in UFO reports and in civilian investigators. How far that interest goes and why it is being kept secret is a matter for speculation among the large number of civilian researchers.

> **'Documents have emerged since by way of leaks and freedom of information requests that show the military is still interested in UFO reports and in civilian investigators.'**

To what extent the military and security services in other countries have been involved in UFO investigations is a matter of dispute. During the Soviet era, all news from communist countries relating to UFOs was subject to strict censorship. Even now it is almost impossible to gain access to files from that period. Since the fall of the Soviet Union in 1991, UFO reports from those countries have largely been made by and to civilians. It is unknown to what extent the military are involved.

The picture is not much clearer in countries such as Britain, France and Germany. In general, the civilian investigators in those countries are not as well financed nor as numerous as they are in the USA. They have been unable to make much headway in uncovering military witnesses who are willing to talk in public, or in persuading their governments to release documents and information. In developing countries civilians and governments alike are less interested in the subject.

That is not to say that civilian researchers have not had any success with uncovering the truth about UFOs and their apparently alien crews.

It was, after all, a civilian who first alerted the world to the existence of flying saucers, as UFOs were then dubbed. Kenneth Arnold first reported a UFO sighting in 1947, and was at once plunged into a maelstrom of media frenzy. He gave numerous interviews about his own sighting, and was contacted by many media outlets wanting his comments and views on new sightings made by others.

It was Arnold who investigated the Maury Island affair later in 1947. He did so, however, only after a publisher offered to pay him. Arnold was, after all, a businessman who had to earn a living. After the Maury Island affair, he went back to running his company manufacturing fire safety equipment. Although Arnold maintained an interest in UFOs until his death in 1984, he had largely dropped out of research into the subject by the mid 1950s.

Arnold's place as the premier authority on flying saucers was rapidly taken by Major Donald Keyhoe.

Keyhoe had been a pilot in the US Marines, but had left after an injury to pursue a career in journalism. He wrote about aircraft subjects as well as producing a few novels that today would be classed as science fiction. During World War II he rejoined the military and served as a trainer, before returning to journalism in 1945.

> **'It soon became clear to him that the military were taking the subject very seriously and that some within the military hierarchy were deeply concerned.'**

In May 1949 he was asked by Ken Purdy, the editor of *True* magazine, to write an article about flying saucers. Not unnaturally, Keyhoe turned to his contacts in the military for help and advice. It soon became clear to him that the military were taking the subject very seriously and that some within the military hierarchy were deeply concerned. This was in the days of Project Sign, and Keyhoe accurately uncovered much of what was going on within the Sign team.

ATOMIC BOMBS AND ALIENS

It was Keyhoe who launched on to the public the suggestion that flying saucers were, in fact, alien spacecraft. The fact that several of the earliest sightings came from the south-western states of the USA caused Keyhoe to suggest that the aliens were primarily interested in the atomic bomb tests that had been carried out there and in the atomic weapons that were stored in the vicinity. Keyhoe thought that the aliens had probably been watching humanity's technological advance since at least the Industrial Revolution, and possibly for some time before that, though he concentrated on events since the first atomic bomb test in 1945.

Keyhoe was responsible for establishing another enduring feature of UFO research when he put forward the idea that senior officials within the USAF knew much more than they were willing to admit. Publicly, Keyhoe based this view on the fact that statements from the USAF were contradictory and incomplete. Privately he said that he had found evidence that there had been a large scale cover-up that had started in 1947.

At this distance in time it is impossible to know quite what Keyhoe uncovered but chose to keep private. Some argue that he was talking about Project Sign and the Estimate of the Situation document that were then being kept secret. Others suspect that he came across the fringes of the Roswell cover-up, but had been unable to discover what real facts lay behind the official smokescreen of denials.

Whatever the truth, Keyhoe wrote his classic magazine article 'The Flying Saucers are Real' for *True* in 1950, and quickly followed it up with a book of the same name. In 1953 he produced a second book,

Flying Saucers From Outer Space, in which he reviewed and publicized some of the best early sightings. Keyhoe went on to produce a string of other books – he did, after all, need to earn a living – but it was an action taken in 1956 that perhaps had a more long-lasting effect.

During the summer of 1956, Keyhoe got to know physicist Townsend Brown. Brown was interested in interstellar travel and thought that a study of UFOs might point towards a possible propulsion system. He had been attending a series of informal

The atomic blast that destroyed Nagasaki in 1945. Many people believe that it was the invention of the atomic bomb that caused aliens to take an interest in Earth.

discussions hosted in Washington DC on the subject. He and Keyhoe formulated the idea of creating a wider, more formal organization with rules and membership fees so that a wider public could discuss the subject.

UFOS FOR ALL

On 24 October the National Investigations Committee on Aerial Phenomena (NICAP) was founded. Brown and Keyhoe were on the board, as was the retired Admiral Delmer Fahrney, along with other senior and respected figures. The idea was that the group would use membership fees and donations to fund serious research. Keyhoe was soon chairing the organization. With a peak membership of 14,000 people, NICAP undertook a good deal of research into UFOs. Witnesses were interviewed, investigations undertaken and copious files maintained.

By 1969, however, membership had fallen to around 5,000 due to the lack of public interest in UFOs after the Condon Committee. NICAP ran into financial problems and Keyhoe resigned as chairman. It has been suggested that CIA infiltration of NICAP at this time was responsible for Keyhoe being forced to resign, and for the subsequent continued decline in membership and finances. NICAP ceased to operate in 1980 and was disbanded.

Keyhoe had meanwhile moved on to help found the Mutual UFO Network (MUFON). This was established as a non-profit corporation and adopted a strictly non-

One of the displays organized by MUFON, one of the most prestigious of the UFO investigation organizations.

sensationalist approach. The organization's emphasis on proper methodology and rational investigations persuaded several respectable scientists to join.

MUFON maintains a network of volunteer investigators across the USA and in some other countries. When a sighting of a UFO is reported in the media, a MUFON investigator is tasked with discovering more details. This may involve merely collecting media reports, but may include interviews with witnesses or detailed on-the-spot investigations depending on the quality of the report and the amount of time the volunteer can spare. At the time of writing in 2008 MUFON is the world's largest UFO investigations group. It maintains an excellent website at www.mufon.com.

In Britain the leading organization is the British UFO Research Association (BUFORA), based in London. This organization maintains a frequently updated website at www.bufora.org.uk. There are numerous smaller, more regional organizations, of which one of the more active is the Birmingham UFO Group, which has its own website at bufogsightings.blogspot.com.

Others active in the UFO field prefer to work largely alone. British researcher Jenny Randles has been a leading light in BUFORA, but is best known for her work when acting alone. It was largely the work of Randles that uncovered the events at Llandrillo in 1974. Nuclear scientist Stanton Friedman was responsible for uncovering the initial discrepancies regarding the alleged crash at Roswell that sparked the interest in the event. He has also produced a range of books that track government cover-ups of UFO-related incidents and facts. Timothy Good has likewise concentrated on government archives and cover-ups.

Lawyer Peter Gersten took on the CIA in 1977 asking it to release documents, and won. He has since been in court many times seeking to persuade government agencies to make their reports available. Darrel Sims was a CIA employee until he suffered an abduction experience and left to investigate the phenomenon that he had experienced himself. He has been especially active in investigating alleged alien implants.

> **'... as he studied increasing numbers of reports he began to change his mind and by the early 1960s came to believe that something truly inexplicable was taking place.'**

A prominent individual researcher, who began working for the USAF but ended up founding a leading UFO study group, was J. Allen Hynek. He founded the Center for UFO Studies (CUFOS), which has a website on www.cufos.org.

Dr J. Allen Hynek was born in 1910 and followed an eminent career path as an academic and practical astronomer. He was called upon by Project Blue Book to advise on astronomy, and in particular whether individual UFO sightings might be mistaken viewings of meteors, comets, planets and other heavenly bodies. At first, Hynek was sceptical about UFOs. He thought that all sightings could be explained away as perfectly normal objects seen in odd circumstances. However, as he studied increasing numbers of reports he began to change his mind and by the early 1960s came to believe that something truly inexplicable was taking place.

HYNEK AND CATEGORIZATION

It was not until the later 1960s that Hynek announced his change of mind in public. In 1972 he published a book, *The UFO Experience*. Stating that the UFO was a real phenomenon and coming as it did from a former pro-government debunker, the book

Jenny Randles, a leading British UFO researcher who has been instrumental in uncovering several key incidents.

caused a sensation. In it Hynek took a restrained view, refusing to endorse the wilder theories and stating only that UFOs were real objects that deserved greater study. The following year he founded CUFOS.

It was Hynek who developed the methods of grading UFO sightings by type that are still in widespread use today. He established three grades of distant sightings: Daylight Discs, Nocturnal Lights and Radar-Visuals. He then categorized three types of Close Encounter. A Close Encounter of the First Kind was when a UFO was seen at such close quarters and in such clear conditions that there could be no doubt as to what was seen. A Close Encounter of the Second Kind was one in which the UFO left behind physical traces, such as burned grass or crushed vegetation. A Close Encounter of the Third Kind occurred when a UFO was seen in conjunction with humanoids or crew.

Hynek went on to act as consultant on the epic 1977 movie *Close Encounters of the Third Kind*. He is usually credited with making sure that the film's

A scene from the movie *Close Encounters of the Third Kind*, the first film to portray UFOs as they are reported by witnesses.

depictions of both UFOs and aliens corresponded closely to the majority of eyewitness reports. The fictional storyline and rather vague ending were not linked to his involvement.

Hynek died in 1986, but before passing away he had co-operated with the French investigator Dr Jacques Vallée in presenting a speech on UFOs to the General Assembly of the United Nations.

Vallée first became interested in UFOs when working as a junior astronomer at the Paris Observatory in the 1960s. He and other youthful colleagues often tracked anomalous objects either in or entering Earth's orbit. When the observatory manager discovered what they were doing he confiscated and destroyed all records of the objects, saying that he feared ridicule from serious astronomers if word leaked out they were doing work on UFOs.

The idea that reported encounters with UFOs and aliens were similar to those that in earlier centuries were interpreted as meetings with fairies or angels was first put forward by French investigator Jacques Vallée.

> **'Vallée advanced the idea that medieval reports of demons, 18th-century encounters with fairies and modern alien abductions were all part of the same phenomenon.'**

Vallée later produced books on UFOs that supported the idea that they were alien spacecraft. By the 1970s, however, Vallée had moved away from the idea that UFOs were machines. Instead he explored the similarities between the reported behaviour of aliens and that of goblins, fairies and demons in earlier centuries. He advanced the idea that medieval reports of demons, 18th-century encounters with fairies and modern alien abductions were all part of the same phenomenon. He argued that the differences in interpretation were caused by the preconceived ideas of the society in which the witness lived, not by any difference in the actual experience.

Exactly what the true face of these aliens/demons/fairies might be is unclear. Vallée himself suggested that they are manifestations of an extremely powerful, non-human but ultimately benign intelligence that seeks to guide humanity along a path to psychic awakening. Others have suggested that the reality is that a human mind given to hallucinations will usually produce similar visions that are then interpreted according to the cultural background of the person doing the hallucinating.

Influential as Vallée's ideas have been in linking the modern UFO experience to earlier encounters between humans and non-human entities, most researchers prefer to stick to the idea that UFOs are ultimately of alien origin.

Just as there have been UFO researchers prepared to accept the reality of the UFO phenomenon, while disagreeing about the explanation, there have been other researchers who remain sceptical.

One of the more active of the early debunkers was Donald Menzel, an American astrophysicist born in 1901 who spent most of his career at Harvard. In 1953 he wrote a book entitled *Flying Saucers* which dismissed all sightings up to that point as being of mundane objects seen in unusual circumstances. He maintained this line in several later books and media appearances. There can be no doubt that his impeccable scientific standing and the trenchant way in which he expressed his opinions did much to influence official views on UFOs. He served as an advisor to the Condon Committee.

Menzel made important contributions to the field of UFO study, although few researchers taking a more pro-UFO stance would thank him. He did correctly identify astronomic explanations for some famous sightings. The peculiar visual effects of atmospheric temperature inversions on stars seen through them, for example, were established by Menzel. He also proved to be adept at suggesting explanations for sightings that were, at least, feasible.

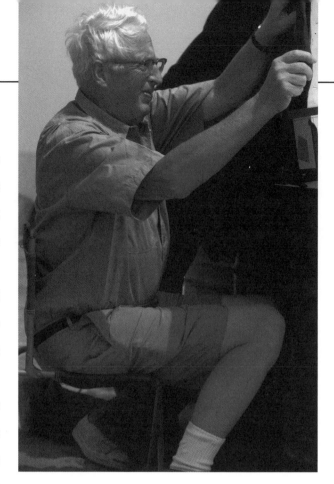

Dr Donald Menzel, an American astrophysicist who has consistently denounced the idea that Earth is being visited by aliens.

Where Menzel proved to be weak was that he very rarely visited the site of a UFO incident or interviewed the witness in person. He tended to produce explanations based on media reports. These sometimes collapsed when further details became available, which served to undermine Menzel's views – at least in the eyes of UFO researchers more willing to accept the phenomenon.

Menzel died in 1976, but others were ready to take up his cause. Perhaps the best known of these has been Philip Klass. An electrical engineer by training, Klass became interested in UFOs in the 1960s and produced a theory that at least some UFO sightings could be explained as being electro-meteorological events such as ball lightning or plasma discharges.

He wrote a book on the subject and gained some fame as a result.

Klass has since stated that most UFO sightings are misidentifications, frauds or hoaxes. Like Menzel before him, Klass has done much in-depth research and has successfully provided mundane explanations for some incidents that at first seemed quite baffling. Also like Menzel, Klass has been accused of sometimes overlooking evidence that does not fit his theories.

Perhaps Klass's most famous contribution to the study of UFOs was his famous '$10,000 Offer' of 1966. This offer was open to anyone who cared to take it up and read as follows:

Klass agrees to pay to the second party the sum of $10,000 within thirty days after any of the following occur:

(A) *Any crashed spacecraft, or major piece of a spacecraft is found to be clearly of extraterrestrial origin by the United States National Academy of Sciences, or*

(B) *The National Academy of Sciences announces that it has examined other evidence which conclusively proves that Earth has been visited by extraterrestrial spacecraft in the 20th century, or*

(C) *A bona fide extraterrestrial visitor, born on a celestial body other than the Earth, appears live before the General Assembly of the United Nations or on a national television program.*

Philip Klass who made the famous '$10,000 Offer' relating to evidence of alien visits to Earth.

* *The party accepting this offer pays Klass $100 per year, for each year none of these things occur.*

So far as is known only one person took up the offer, paying Klass the agreed $100 per year. At the time of Klass's death in 2005 the prize was unclaimed.

No event met Klass's criteria, but that does not mean that UFOs are not real. There is plenty of evidence to indicate that they are genuine. The question is, what are they and why are they here?

CHAPTER 7
GOVERNMENT COVER-UPS

A motel in Nevada, close to the highly secretive Area 51, uses an alien to appeal to passing customers.

An aspect of the UFO experience that has been of increasing importance in recent years is the stories and allegations of government cover-ups and deliberate lies.

Undoubtedly the governments of several nations have set out to mislead the public over UFOs. They have dismissed sightings without any real evidence, have sought to discredit witnesses and have generally undermined research into the subject. Although some governments, that of the USA and UK in particular, have recently released documents that were previously kept secret and have made efforts to explain their previous clandestine activities were due to Cold War suspicions, it is clear that many other documents remain classified and out of the sight of the public.

Several theories have been advanced to account for the evidence of government secrecy. The starting point for most of these are the reports of UFO crashes of the later 1940s and early 1950s. The Roswell Crash of July 1947 is the best known of these alleged events. There is enough evidence relating to the Roswell Crash to indicate that something strange did come down in the desert. The Invasion Hypothesis holds that it was an alien spacecraft, and that the dead crew were inside it.

Opinion among UFO researchers is more divided over the Aztec Crash, the Paradise Valley Crash, the Laredo Crash and others. Some believe that most if not all of these events were real UFO crashes. Under this scenario it is thought that there was a covert war going on between the USAF and the mysterious intruders. The reported loss of several aircraft and UFOs in a short period of time would indicate that some sort of hostile action was taking place. That the series of crashes ended in the early 1950s would indicate that the hostilities ended.

> **'The reported loss of several aircraft and UFOs in a short period of time would indicate that some sort of hostile action was taking place.'**

Other researchers view the rash of poorly documented UFO crashes quite differently. They see the reports, all made with little supporting evidence, as signs of a cover-up. This scenario envisages the Roswell Crash as being the only genuine event that saw the USAF retrieve a crashed UFO and its crew. The decision was then made by the USAF high command that it would be almost impossible to keep such an event entirely out of the public view, especially as a press release had been issued from the base before the news blackout was imposed.

The false stories of crashes elsewhere were therefore concocted and spread as a smokescreen. The USAF could then dismiss the reports of the Roswell Crash on the grounds that the other crash reports had all turned out to be bogus, implying that the Roswell Crash was no different.

Both schools of thought agree that the Roswell wreckage, and possibly that of other crashed UFOs, was taken to the Wright-Patterson Air Force Base. This high security facility is strictly guarded and news of what goes on there is classified to the highest levels. All that can be said with certainty is that it houses a number of specialist technical departments of the USAF, of which one is the Foreign Technology Division (FTD). The FTD examines any weapons or military technology captured from enemy nations during wartime, or acquired by secret agents.

THE BLUE ROOM AND AREA 51

If any UFO technology had been captured it would almost certainly go to the FTD for analysis. According to information gained from ex-workers at Wright-Patterson, there exists a section of such high security that only a handful of the most senior staff are allowed access, and even they under very strict conditions. This section goes by various names such as the Blue Room, Hangar 18 or Building 18-F. It is here that the UFO wreckage is said to be stored.

In 1962 Senator Barry Goldwater, at that time chairman of the Senate Intelligence Committee, asked to enter the Blue Room. He was refused permission by General Curtis LeMay on the grounds of military security. The event at least proved that the secret room exists, but does not necessarily prove that it houses a UFO.

The Blue Room and its alleged contents have featured in a number of fictional Hollywood movies. Perhaps the best known was the 1980 movie *Hangar 18*. By the time *Independence Day,* the big-budget blockbuster about an alien invasion, was made in 1996, the Blue Room had been superseded in UFO research circles by rumours about Area 51.

Like Wright-Patterson, Area 51 undoubtedly exists. It covers a vast area of desert and near-desert land in Nevada, close to the dry lake bed known as Lake Groom. What goes on there is also known in outline. It is where the USAF tests new aircraft and new military electronics equipment of various kinds, as well as new weaponry. The base is, understandably, cloaked in the strictest secrecy. For many years, the USAF refused to admit that the place existed and the base was not even shown on maps.

During the 1980s the existence of Area 51 was officially admitted. This led to numerous aircraft enthusiasts visiting the area to climb hills that gave

views over the base. Worried that the visitors might include foreign agents, the USAF bought several square miles of land around the base and brought it into the security zone. No vantage points were left accessible to the public. It was about this time that rumours began to circulate that the contents of the Blue Room had been moved to Area 51.

> **'In 1962 Senator Barry Goldwater ... chairman of the Senate Intelligence Committee, asked to enter the Blue Room. He was refused permission ... on the grounds of military security.'**

The rumours were in part prompted by an informant who claimed to be a technician formerly employed at Area 51. At first using a false name, 'Dennis', the informant identified himself in 1989 as Robert Lazar. Lazar was an electronics engineer and computer expert from California. According to his evidence, Lazar was approached by Naval Intelligence and asked to work on a top secret project. He and other technicians were driven in a bus with blacked out windows to a desert site that he only later identified as Area 51. There he was given some highly sophisticated electronic equipment and told to figure out how it worked and how replicas could be built. The process, known as reverse-engineering, is well established but Lazar claimed the equipment he

Myrna Hanssen reported that the aliens who abducted her were performing bizarre and painful experiments on cattle.

handled was so advanced and bizarre that he soon concluded that it must be of alien origin.

Lazar claimed that his suspicions were confirmed when he confronted the head of the project with his conclusions. He was later allowed to see a large room that contained a variety of wreckage and artefacts. One UFO was intact, consisting of a 35 ft (10 m) diameter disc of sleek lines. Lazar claims that technicians at Area 51 had worked out how to make the UFO hover briefly, but had not mastered how to make it fly.

ELEMENT 115

The UFO was kept in the air by a process described to Lazar as 'gravity amplification'. The main component in this technology was the substance 'Element 115',

with an atomic weight of 115. This would make the atom of the material excessively heavy, indeed heavier than any element known on Earth. All heavy elements on Earth are unstable and prone to radioactive decay, but Lazar insisted that on the contrary, Element 115 was very stable. More recent physics theory suggests that theoretical elements of a weight above 110 may indeed be stable. Some take this to be evidence that Lazar had been privy to secret alien technology.

Be that as it may, Lazar said that the reason he went public was that he had been threatened by USAF officers after he insisted on leaving the project. He was, he said, in fear of his life and decided that by telling all he knew he would remove any motive the authorities had for killing him.

Not everyone took Lazar's evidence seriously, especially after it emerged that he had been in trouble with the law in the early 1980s. Sceptics argued that with all the electronics experts in the USA to choose from, the authorities were unlikely to select a man convicted of criminal activities to work on a top secret project.

Lazar was not the only source for information indicating that the USAF had alien spaceships on its bases. Dr Paul Bennewitz was the owner of an electronics company in Albuquerque, New Mexico, who in 1980 began picking up a series of highly unusual electromagnetic signals. These began during a time when local people reported seeing several UFOs near the town. Bennewitz phoned the USAF and spoke to Major Ernest Edwards about his findings.

'... using the electromagnetic signals to identify UFOs and plot their courses, he found that they appeared to be landing and taking off from the nearby USAF base of Sandia.'

Bennewitz set about trying to track the UFOs, using the electromagnetic signals to identify them and plot their courses. He found that they appeared to be landing and taking off from the nearby USAF base of Sandia. This base was, and remains, a top secret installation involved with atomic weapon storage and maintenance. Edwards had meanwhile

passed Bennewitz's concerns on, which resulted in personnel being sent to see Bennewitz with the express intention of persuading him to halt his investigations. They explained to him that he had picked up signals being generated by a top secret research project that had nothing to do with UFOs. Bennewitz did not believe the claims and instead contacted William Moore, a noted UFO researcher.

The two men investigated other New Mexico UFO incidents, in particularly the abduction of Myrna Hanssen near Cimarron. Hanssen recounted under regressive hypnosis how she had been abducted by a group of greys, along with her son and a hapless nearby cow. The cow was mutilated while still alive, causing understandable fear in Hanssen as to the fate in store for her and her son.

The greys were then interrupted by a tall, more human figure who apologized to the woman and told her that her abduction had been a mistake. The alien said that Hanssen would be taken to the alien base while the matter was sorted out. The two humans were then escorted to a vast underground complex. Once there, she escaped from her captors. She fled to a room in which were a number of vats or barrels, each filled with a viscous liquid in which floated human body parts. Hanssen was recaptured, her memory wiped and she and her son returned to Earth's surface.

Bennewitz's work convinced him that the aliens were working alongside the USAF. He located the underground base as being in the region of, and perhaps directly beneath, the USAF base at Dulce, New Mexico. Other researchers think that the evidence points more towards the Superstition Mountains of Arizona.

ALIENS IN THE USAF?

In 1983 a former USAF security officer named Thomas Castello approached Bennewitz with what he claimed were photocopies of highly classified documents that he had stolen when working at the USAF Dulce base. These documents revealed that beneath Dulce was a seven-level deep research facility. The four levels closest to ground level were run by USAF personnel. The fifth level was a transition zone where human officials met and worked with aliens, while the sixth and seventh levels were staffed entirely by aliens.

The alien staff were said to number around 15,000 greys, together with a few hundred reptiloid aliens known as the draco. The experiments these aliens undertook were based on genetics and aimed at producing not only genetically modified trans-species organisms but also at separating the human's 'bioplasmic body' from the physical body. Castello speculated that the phrase bioplasmic body meant the soul.

Some suspect that there are several bases excavated under the Earth's surface. One such is often said to be at Santiago in Puerto Rico. A US army base at Santiago is located close to the area where

'The four levels closest to ground level were run by USAF personnel. The fifth level was a transition zone where human officials met and worked with aliens, while the sixth and seventh levels were staffed entirely by aliens.'

several witnesses have seen UFOs entering and leaving what appears to be an underground hangar. The doors to the hangar are about 80 ft (24 m) in size, made of metal and camouflaged with rocks, bushes and soil.

Claims similar to those made for Dulce have been put forward for an alleged alien headquarters under the USAF base at Montauk, New York State. These claims come mostly from Preston Nichols, a researcher into ESP who claims to have recovered memories of his time working at Montauk where he supervised investigations into time travel using a hyperspatial time tunnel.

Meanwhile, Bennewitz suffered a nervous breakdown in 1986 and withdrew from UFO research, leaving William Moore to work on alone. Moore, and other researchers, received in the post from an anonymous source documents that claimed to come from an organization named 'Majestic 12' (MJ12). The earliest documents were dated 18 November 1952 and they promised to solve the whole UFO riddle.

The MJ12 documents claimed to be the records of a top secret group set up by President Truman to

US President Harry Truman was in office at the time of the alleged Roswell Crash and would have taken the decisions about how the government should react.

A full-scale alien invasion, in collaboration with government organizations, could spell the end for the majority of mankind.

study alien artefacts recovered from a crashed UFO. Although the place where this UFO crashed is not stated, evidence in the documents points to Roswell. The Majestic 12 documents set out how the public are to be misled by disinformation programmes filtered through Project Blue Book and friendly journalists, while the real work of reverse engineering the alien technology would proceed at Wright-Patterson.

All the people named in the documents were high ranking military or government officials who held positions that would have put them in a position to be involved in any study of UFOs. The paper on which the documents are typed is correct for the era they purport to come from, the typewriter used is of a type used in the Pentagon in the 1950s and there is nothing to indicate the papers are forgeries.

'The more involved theories arising from the MJ12 documents and what they claim to prove state that the Roswell Crash of 1947 led to negotiations being opened between the US government and the aliens.'

The more involved theories arising from the MJ12 documents and what they claim to prove state that the Roswell Crash of 1947 led to negotiations being opened between the US government and the aliens. These resulted in a treaty being agreed that led to the construction by the aliens of the vast underground bases at Dulce, Montauk and elsewhere. In return for access to advanced alien technology, the US government agreed that the aliens could abduct humans deemed suitable for their experiments.

Some claim that the US government is now secretly working on weapons and technologies that would enable Earth to withstand an attack by the aliens, should they turn hostile. Others claim that the supposed weapons-development programme

has been prompted by the fact that the aliens have already broken the treaty by abducting more humans than had been agreed. Still others think that the US government is engaged with the aliens on a project called 'Alternative 3'. This project involves the construction on Mars, or some other planet, of a colony to which selected humans could escape when a disaster that the aliens have predicted overwhelms the Earth. Only a few humans would escape – most of them US government officials and their families – the rest of humanity being left to die. Such conspiracies are not mentioned in the MJ12 documents, but have come from other sources and are now believed by a growing minority of UFO researchers.

If the MJ12 documents are real, they prove not only that UFOs exist, but that they are alien spacecraft and that the US government has been covering up the truth for decades. Some researchers hold them to be genuine and to be the ultimate proof of what has been going on for all these years.

Others are suspicious of the fact that the documents came from an anonymous source. They are, it is said, too good to be true. Although there is no proof to denounce the MJ12 documents, most researchers think they are forgeries.

As with so much about the whole UFO phenomenon, the truth about the MJ12 documents turns out to be a matter of opinion. So does any attempt to draw conclusions about the subject.

CONCLUSION

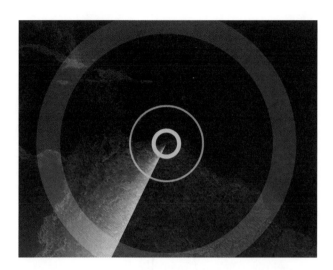

Several UFOs have shown up on radar traces, indicating that whatever they are, they are solid enough to reflect radar waves.

The UFO phenomenon is clearly not so much a single puzzle as several. There are many different pieces to the jigsaw, and it is not always clear how they fit together. There are sightings of UFOs, sometimes at very close range and supported by radar evidence. There are claims that UFOs have crashed and been retrieved by government organizations. There are witnesses who report seeing humanoids emerging from UFOs or flying off in them. There are contactees who report having met and spoken with benevolent aliens from other planets. And there are abductees whose contact with apparent aliens is altogether more disturbing and sinister.

Sceptics tend to concentrate their explanations on sightings of UFOs. They explain these away as sightings of stars, meteors, aircraft and other mundane aerial objects seen under bizarre conditions. When they pay any attention at all to claims of sightings and encounters with aliens – which is not often – they dismiss them as hallucinations, dreams and fraud.

Even among UFO researchers who accept that there is some anomalous phenomenon to investigate, there is no consensus as to what should be taken seriously and what should not. There are some who believe that UFOs are alien spaceships, but then dismiss the claims of contactees as hoaxes designed to earn money through publicity. There are those who believe that aliens visit Earth, but discount abductions as being a psychological phenomenon rather than an objective reality.

It is a real challenge to get behind the reports to discover the truth, but any researcher needs to make the effort if they are to make sense of the UFO phenomenon.

As a starting point, it is necessary to review a summary of what is known about the various different phenomena related to UFOs. It is not so much in the spectacular and unique events that the underlying reality is to be found. It is more likely that the true face of what is going on will be discovered by

'When they pay any attention at all to claims of sightings of aliens – which is not often – they dismiss them as hallucinations, dreams and fraud.'

A typical UFO as described by witnesses is round, metallic and has a dome on top.

looking at the vast mass of data relating to more numerous but less dramatic sightings and events. Some deductions can be made from these to reach a composite image of what is being encountered.

Starting with UFOs themselves, it is safe to draw some conclusions. The first is that the majority of sightings of unidentified flying objects are, in fact, of perfectly normal things that simply have not been identified by the witness. There are, however, many thousands of reports of sightings that exhibit features that cannot possibly be explained away in terms of normal objects.

These objects tend to be between 30 and 100 ft (9 and 30 m) in size. They have smoothly rounded outlines, often with a dome on top, and no obvious joints, seams or other features. When seen in daylight they appear to be made of a silvery metallic material, though there are often transparent 'windows' inserted into the craft. When seen at night they

'There are, however, many thousands of reports of sightings that exhibit features that cannot possibly be explained away in terms of normal objects.'

pulsate with light that changes colour with some frequency. There are often small lights set around the rim of the craft. The objects may move silently, but at other times emit a hum or buzzing sound.

These objects have been observed to have a distinct impact on their surroundings. Vegetation may be flattened if a UFO rests on the ground, or pushed aside as one flies by. Plants may also show signs of scorching if they come into contact with a UFO. Electrical equipment, such as radios and car ignition systems, can be affected by a UFO in close proximity. They are capable of exceptionally high speeds and sudden changes of direction that are well outside the range of abilities of human-built aircraft.

It seems reasonable to assume that these UFOs are solid objects. The impact on things around them would indicate that they emit strong heat, as well as magnetic and electrical fields. Some observed effects would support a radioactive source being located within the UFO.

The humanoids that are reported to emerge from UFOs also have features in common. These figures are generally less than 5 ft (1.5 m) in height, sometimes considerably smaller. They are basically humanoid, but often have abnormally large bald heads. They typically wear one-piece suits and sometimes helmets. The humanoids are usually described as being very curious about their surroundings, collecting samples of plants and soil or studying animals. They will look about in buildings and seem intrigued by devices such as cars or furniture.

When they become aware that a human is observing them they typically get back into their UFO and fly off at speed. Occasionally they will react to a human by temporarily paralyzing or dazzling them. This seems to be designed to allow the aliens to escape and no lasting damage is done to the human.

'Any discrepancies in the descriptions of the humanoids by witnesses – and there are many – are usually said to be due to the shock of what they have seen.'

There is nothing about these humanoids to indicate that they are from another planet, other than their anomalous nature.

These beings behave very much like secretive explorers. They seem to be interested in all forms of life on Earth, but do not want to be discovered by or have any form of contact with humans. Any discrepancies in the descriptions of the humanoids by witnesses – and there are many – are usually said to be due to the shock of what they have seen. The witness, it is said, is so astonished by what is happening that they take in only part of the whole scenario and so pass on details and features that do not always match exactly with those reported by other witnesses.

The aliens reported by contactees are almost always very much more human than the beings that emerge from landed UFOs, but flee without conversing. These aliens are often likened to perfect humans, with descriptions of astonishing beauty and

Many UFO reports speak of automobiles being controlled by spacecraft or of aliens equipped with devices that can paralyze humans.

great intelligence being usual. These aliens usually converse quite normally with the witness. They claim to be friendly and often warn of some impending disaster of a vast but unspecified nature. They do, however, make statements that frequently turn out not to be true.

Taken at face value, these aliens are super-intelligent representatives of a highly developed interplanetary civilization that is well disposed to humanity. It is noteworthy that they tend to make contact with relatively unimportant people rather than with leading political figures or high ranking military officers. The fact that they also make misleading and untrue statements has led some researchers to believe that these aliens are tricksters who delight in misleading humans. Others think that the contactees are either hoaxers or have hallucinated their experiences.

WHAT ARE THEY AND WHY ARE THEY HERE?

The creatures that carry out abductions are generally of the type now known as greys. They are short and have abnormally large heads. Unlike the humanoids that emerge from landed UFOs, however, they do not generally wear clothes nor are they interested in plants and animals. They most certainly do not flee when humans are observed. Instead these creatures seem obsessed with humans, and in particular with their physiology and reproductive systems. They carry out medical examinations and procedures that are often extremely painful, but of uncertain purpose. These creatures seem to treat humans with total indifference, much as a human scientist might treat a laboratory rat.

In a very few instances, these greys communicate with their victims, and then it is usually by telepathy. They indicate that they are from another star system, though how much trust should be put in communications from such a source is uncertain. Abductions are sometimes, but not always, linked to sightings of a UFO.

The greys seem to be conducting research and experimentation on humans. This appears to be focused on breeding and, at least according to some witnesses, involves producing human-alien hybrids. Some researchers note that the greys routinely try to wipe the memories of their victims and conclude that the aliens want to carry out their experiments in

> 'These creatures seem to treat humans with total indifference, much as a human scientist might treat a laboratory rat.'

secret. A few researchers treat the abduction experience with caution, pointing out that some features of it have much in common with dreams and the human unconscious.

The most widely accepted theory to account for all this information is that the UFOs are spacecraft from another planet and that the humanoids that emerge from them are their alien crews. Why the aliens are coming to Earth is another matter entirely, and opinions are divided.

The behaviour of those emerging from UFOs would seem to indicate that the mission is primarily scientific and – at least at this stage – non-hostile. The greys, on the other hand, appear to be more inclined to interfere with humans and perhaps even with human evolution.

Since investigations into UFOs began to be taken seriously by the various civilian organizations in the later 1950s, a mass of evidence has emerged that would indicate that the aliens are here in numbers

> 'The behaviour of those emerging from UFOs would seem to indicate that the mission is primarily scientific and – at least at this stage – non-hostile.'

'The theory that Earth is being visited by races of beings from a highly advanced interplanetary civilization is certainly extraordinary.'

and that they are acting in co-operation with one or more Earth governments. How much of that evidence should be taken seriously, how much discarded and what it all means is a matter for dispute. It does, however, form the basis of what might be termed the Invasion Hypothesis.

This hypothesis takes as its starting point that UFOs are alien spaceships. The aliens themselves are generally held to be greys. The humanoids sighted behaving in more benign ways near landed UFOs are assumed to be greys engaged on more mundane missions and not directly active in abductions. The aliens reported by contactees are not included in this theory and are discounted as hoaxes or hallucinations.

Extraordinary theories require extraordinary proof, so goes an accepted rule of thumb in conventional science. The theory that Earth is being visited by races of beings from a highly advanced interplanetary civilization is certainly extraordinary. Has extraordinary proof been put forward to support the theory?

Quite obviously the answer to that question is a simple 'no'. No alien has landed his spaceship on the lawn outside the White House, in Moscow's Red Square or at London's Downing Street. Still less has such an alien strolled out to demand: 'Take me to your leader.'

But that would presuppose that the alien in question wanted to meet our leader and, indeed, that he was happy for humans to know that he was here.

What if our theoretical alien did not want humans to know that he was visiting Earth? What if his purpose on our planet depended on humans being unaware of his existence, or at least unwilling to accept its reality? Then the alien would come secretly, land in out-of-the-way places and seek to avoid human contact unless he himself controlled it in every way. And that is exactly how the humanoids associated with UFOs are reported to behave.

'... the way the US and other governments have engaged in programmes of misinformation, cover-ups and spurious denials is exactly how a government would behave if it were hiding some dark secret.'

It has similarly never been proved that the US government is actively engaged in working with the aliens. Such theories rest on evidence that is often controversial, and itself rests on theories and suppositions as much as on the unsupported word of individuals. But again, the way the US and other governments have engaged in programmes of

Science fiction movies frequently show UFOs touching down next to landmarks, such as the White House. In reality UFOs prefer remote locations. Perhaps they do not want the publicity that a call on the US President would generate.

misinformation, cover-ups and spurious denials is exactly how a government would behave if it were hiding some dark secret.

This does not necessarily prove that they are aliens, still less why they are here. The evidence available falls short of the extraordinary proof needed to demonstrate an extraordinary theory. But they do go far beyond the levels of proof needed to show conclusively that something is going on.

People do see UFOs of a size, type and performance that mean that they cannot be man-made or natural objects. Witnesses do undoubtedly see humanoids emerging from these UFOs. Reputable people are seeing them still.

Whether these creatures go by the name of goblin, fairy or alien, they have been seen by thousands of credible and reliable people. Perhaps time will tell what they are and why they are here.

INDEX